# CHRIST HUMBLED
# YET EXALTED

# CHRIST HUMBLED YET EXALTED

John Flavel

Abridged by
J. Stephen Yuille

**Reformation Heritage Books**
Grand Rapids, Michigan

*Christ Humbled yet Exalted*
© 2021 by Reformation Heritage Books

**Reformation Heritage Books**
3070 29th St. SE
Grand Rapids, MI 49512
616-977-0889
orders@heritagebooks.org
www.heritagebooks.org

*Printed in the United States of America*
21 22 23 24 25 26/10 9 8 7 6 5 4 3 2 1

Library of Congress Cataloging-in-Publication Data

Names: Flavel, John, 1630?-1691, author. | Yuille, J. Stephen, 1968- editor.
Title: Christ humbled yet exalted / John Flavel ; abridged by J. Stephen Yuille.
Description: Grand Rapids, Michigan : Reformation Heritage Books, [2021] | Includes bibliographical references.
Identifiers: LCCN 2021008175 (print) | LCCN 2021008176 (ebook) | ISBN 9781601788511 (paperback) | ISBN 9781601788528 (epub)
Subjects: LCSH: Jesus Christ—Humiliation. | Jesus Christ—Exaltation.
Classification: LCC BT222 .F53 2021  (print) | LCC BT222  (ebook) | DDC 232/.8—dc23
LC record available at https://lccn.loc.gov/2021008175
LC ebook record available at https://lccn.loc.gov/2021008176

*For additional Reformed literature, request a free book list from Reformation Heritage Books at the above regular or email address.*

# Contents

# Preface

"For those who believe unto the saving of the soul," writes John Owen, "Christ is precious—the sun, the rock, the life, the bread of their souls—everything that is good, useful, amiable, desirable, here or unto eternity."[1] When Adam and Eve disobeyed in the garden, they—along with all their posterity—fell into bondage to sin and death. On the cross, however, Christ bore God's judgment in our place. We enter into the blessings of His substitutionary sacrifice when we believe in Him. He unites us to Himself by the Holy Spirit, whereby we enjoy all that He purchased for us. This makes Christ *precious* beyond compare (Phil. 3:8). As John Flavel declares,

> Lord, the condemnation was Yours, that the justification might be mine. The agony was Yours, that the victory might be mine. The pain was Yours, and the ease mine. The stripes were Yours, and healing balm issuing from them mine. The vinegar and gall were Yours, that the honey and sweet might be mine. The curse was Yours, that the blessing might be mine. The crown of thorns

---

1. John Owen, *The Works of John Owen*, ed. W. H. Gould (London: Johnstone & Hunter, 1850; repr., Edinburgh: Banner of Truth, 1977), 1:3.

was Yours, that the crown of glory might be mine. The death was Yours, but the life purchased by it mine. You paid the price that I might enjoy the inheritance.[2]

Flavel was one of the most popular preachers among the seventeenth-century English Puritans.[3] By the time of his death in 1691, he had ministered for over forty years. "I could say much, though not enough, of the excellency of his preaching," writes one of his congregants, adding, "that person must have a very soft head, or a very hard heart, or both, that could sit under his ministry unaffected."[4] Thankfully, Flavel gave a considerable amount of his time to writing and publishing his sermons. These were compiled after his death, and

---

2. John Flavel, *The Works of John Flavel* (London: W. Baynes and Son, 1820; repr., London: Banner of Truth, 1968) 1:101.

3. For details of Flavel's life, see *The Life of the Late Rev. Mr. John Flavel, Minister of Dartmouth*, in *Works*, 1:i–xvi; and *Dictionary of National Biography*, ed. S. Lee (London: Smith, Elder 1909). Flavel is the subject of the following PhD dissertations: Kawi Chang, "John Flavel of Dartmouth, 1630–1691" (University of Edinburgh, 1952); John Thomas Jr., "An Analysis of the Use of Application in the Preaching of John Flavel" (New Orleans Baptist Theological Seminary, 2007); Brian H. Cosby, "The Theology of Suffering and Sovereignty as Seen in the Writings and Ministry of John Flavel, c. 1630–1691" (Australian College of Theology, 2012); Nathan Thomas Parker, "Proselytization and Apocalypticism in the British Atlantic World—The Theology of John Flavel" (Durham University, 2013). In addition to these dissertations, there are several books on Flavel: Adam Embry, *Keeper of the Great Seal of Heaven: Sealing of the Spirit in the Life and Thought of John Flavel* (Grand Rapids: Reformation Heritage, 2011); J. Stephen Yuille, *The Inner Sanctum of Puritan Piety: John Flavel's Doctrine of Mystical Union with Christ* (Grand Rapids: Reformation Heritage, 2007); Brian H. Cosby, *John Flavel: Puritan Life and Thought in Stuart England* (Lanham, Md.: Lexington Books, 2014); Clifford B. Boone, *Puritan Evangelism: Preaching for Conversion in Late-Seventeenth Century English Puritanism as Seen in the Works of John Flavel* (Milton Keynes, UK: Paternoster, 2013).

4. As quoted in Flavel, *Works*, 1:vi.

his complete works were printed five times in the eighteenth century and multiple times in the nineteenth and twentieth centuries. Some of his books have become classics: *The Foun-tain of Life*, *The Method of Grace*, *The Mystery of Providence*, and *Keeping the Heart*. Each demonstrates his commitment to doctrinal instruction and pastoral application. It has been said that "there are few writers of a more experimental, affection-ate, practical, popular, and edifying character than Flavel."[5]

Much of Flavel's appeal is explained by his familiarity with life's manifold sorrows and sufferings. He ministered out of his experience of great personal loss. His parents died of the plague, contracted while imprisoned for nonconformity.[6] He buried his first three wives along with several children.[7] He was ejected for nonconformity in 1662, exiled by the Five Mile Act in 1665, and generally harassed throughout his ministry. On one occasion, he managed to escape arrest by plunging his horse over a cliff into the sea and swimming to

---

5. Edward Bickersteth, as quoted in Iain Murray, "John Flavel," *Banner of Truth*, no. 60 (September 1968): 3–5.

6. In 1662, Parliament passed an Act of Uniformity according to which all who had not received Episcopal ordination had to be reordained by bish-ops. In addition, ministers had to declare their consent to the entire Book of Common Prayer and their rejection of the Solemn League and Covenant. As a result, approximately two thousand ministers left the Church of England. They became known as "dissenters" or "nonconformists." Flavel's father, Richard, pas-tored a small group of dissenting Christians in London in 1655. In the middle of a prayer meeting, soldiers entered and arrested a number of the participants, including Richard and his wife. Sadly, they contracted the plague while in prison and died shortly after their release.

7. Flavel's first wife, Joan Randall, died while giving birth. Their child also died. His second wife, Elizabeth Stapell, died. They had two children. His third wife, Ann Downs, with whom he also had two children, died. His fourth wife, Dorothy Jeffries, survived him.

shore. Factoring in the strain of demanding pastoral duties
and wearying doctrinal disputes, coupled with the challenges
of living without modern comforts and amenities, Flavel was
deeply acquainted with affliction.

By his own account, it was "joy" that "upheld and for-
tified" him throughout life's arduous journey.[8] He defined
Christian joy as "the cheerfulness of our heart in God"
arising from "the sense of our interest in Him and His
promises."[9] Flavel was convinced that joy is ultimately rooted
in the knowledge of Jesus Christ. "All the comforts of believers," says he, "are streams from this fountain."[10] Again, "Take
away the knowledge of Christ, and a Christian is the most sad
and melancholy creature in the world. Let Christ but manifest Himself, and dart the beams of His light into their souls,
it will make them kiss the stakes, sing in flames, and shout
in the pangs of death."[11] Persuaded of this, Flavel emphasized
the importance of cultivating the knowledge of Christ in the
soul. "All other knowledge, however pleasant and profitable,
is not worthy to be named in the same sentence with the
knowledge of Christ."[12]

This conviction is on full display in the present work:
*Christ Humbled yet Exalted: The Fountain of Life, Part 2*.[13]
Here Flavel demonstrates that Christ is the fountain of true

---

8. Flavel, *Works*, 2:244–45.

9. Flavel, *Works*, 4:429.

10. Flavel, *Works*, 1:35.

11. Flavel, *Works*, 1:35.

12. Flavel, *Works*, 1:34.

13. It is found in Flavel, *Works*, vol. 1. Flavel's original work (*The Fountain of Life*) is a collection of over forty sermons, celebrating Christ from His prein-
carnate glory through His incarnation to His postresurrection glory.

joy because He has secured it for His people by means of His twofold estate—humiliation and exaltation.

When Flavel speaks of Christ's humiliation, he is thinking of His incarnation. "It is a great wonder that God should dwell in a body of flesh (John 1:14), that the eternal God should be born in time, that the Ancient of Days should be as an infant of days. For the infinite glorious Creator of all things to become a creature is a mystery exceeding all human understanding."[14] When the Son of God emptied Himself (Phil. 2:8), He did not cease to be who He is (God) but rather took to Himself the very opposite—human nature (body and soul). He hid His heavenly glory (John 17:5) and gave up the independent exercise of His authority (John 5:30). He emptied Himself of these things with reference to His human nature, not His divine nature. He grew in wisdom and stature yet possessed all knowledge and wisdom. He was hungry and weary yet was all-sufficient and self-sufficient.

For Flavel, Christ's humiliation reached even lower than His incarnation (in itself) to His crucifixion. "And being found in fashion as a man, he humbled himself, and became obedient unto death, even the death of the cross" (Phil. 2:8). The cross marks the lowest point in Christ's humiliation because it is there that He was "made a curse for us: for it is written, Cursed is every one that hangeth on a tree'" (Gal. 3:13). Flavel remarks, "The symbol of suspending [Christ] between heaven and earth carries much shame in it, for it implies that He was so vile that He no longer deserved to touch the surface of the earth. And the command to bury Him the same day implied

---

14. Flavel, *Works*, 1:226.

that He was such an abominable sight that He was to be
removed as soon as possible from before the eyes of others."[15]

Turning to Christ's second estate (exaltation), Flavel
unpacks its four stages: Christ's resurrection from the dead,
ascension into heaven, session at God's right hand, and return
in judgment. As Flavel explains, this exaltation is of funda-
mental importance to Christ's work as mediator:

> Christ's work was not finished on earth in His state of
> suffering and affliction. His exaltation was necessary for
> the completion of His work.... In the Old Testament,
> it was not enough to kill the sacrifice thereby shedding
> its blood. After this was done, the blood had to be car-
> ried through the veil into the most holy place before the
> Lord (Heb. 9:7). So, the shedding of Christ's blood on
> earth would not have been enough unless He had car-
> ried it into heaven, and there performed His work of
> intercession for us.[16]

According to Flavel, Christ's intercession is the means by
which the benefits of His oblation are applied to His people.
He "acted the first part on earth, in a state of deep abasement,
in the form of a servant; but He acts this in glory...that He
may fulfill His design in dying, and give the work of our salvation its last completing act."[17]

By virtue of His twofold estate (humiliation and exaltation), Christ is the foundation of our joy. He has removed our
debt and secured our inheritance. For Flavel, this inheritance

---

15. Flavel, *Works*, 1:323.

16. Flavel, *Works*, 1:170.

17. Flavel, *Works*, 1:166.

is principally the enjoyment of God. This is a present reality in the practice of spiritual duties whereby the Holy Spirit stirs our affections, thereby drawing us to God. Ultimately, however, the full enjoyment of our inheritance awaits us in heaven. "The believer knows," says Flavel, "that however sweet his communion with Christ is in this world, yet that communion he will have with Christ in heaven will far excel it.[18] As Flavel makes clear, the presence of sin disrupts our enjoyment of God at present. At glorification, however, we will be free from this burden. We will be like Christ and therefore able to commune with God to the fullest capacity of our souls. This will result in unparalleled delight as we rest fully in Him. "What is the life of glory but the vision of God, and the soul's assimilation to God by that vision? From both of these results that unspeakable joy and delight which passes understanding."[19]

We see God at present through the eyes of faith,[20] but this is nothing compared to what we will see in heaven. Flavel remarks, "To see God in His Word and works is the happiness of the saints on earth, but to see Him face to face will be the fullness of their blessedness in heaven."[21] As for what it means to see God face to face, Flavel says it is "to know Him as He is…to see Him so perfectly and fully that the understanding can proceed no farther in point of knowledge concerning that

18. Flavel, *Works*, 6:450.

19. Flavel, *Works*, 2:95.

20. According to Flavel, people see Christ in three ways: (1) They see Him "carnally" with an eye of "flesh" (Isa. 53:2); (2) they see Him "fiducially" by the eye of "faith" (John 6:40); and (3) they see Him "beatifically" by the "glorified" eye (Job 19:26–27). Flavel, *Works*, 6:411–12.

21. Flavel, *Works*, 2:282.

great question, *What is God?*[22] For Flavel, this is not primarily
a sight of the eye, but a sight of the soul. In short, the beatific
vision means that the image of God will be restored in us. The
faculties of the soul will again be marked by knowledge, righteousness, and holiness. The mind will perceive God as the
greatest good, and the affections will love God as the greatest good. God will impress His glory on the soul to its fullest
capacity, whereby we make suitable returns to Him.

These "returns" are summed up in the enjoyment of
God. According to Flavel, there is a threefold happiness to
be enjoyed in heaven. The "objective" happiness is God Himself.[23] If He were to offer us heaven without Him, we "would
fall a weeping," declaring, "it is no heaven to us unless You
are there." The "subjective" happiness is the "suiting" of our
soul and body to God. All that is "inconsistent" with a state
of glory will be removed.[24] The "formal" happiness is "the
fullness of satisfaction resulting from the blessed sight and
enjoyment of God." "Ah, what a happiness is here! To look
and love, to drink and sing, and drink again at the fountain
head of the highest glory!"[25] We will find our complete rest in
God, and this will be our heaven.[26] In short, our inheritance
is God, in whose "presence is fulness of joy" and in whose
"right hand there are pleasures for evermore" (Ps. 16:11).

This is what Christ has purchased for us by means of His
twofold estate of humiliation and exaltation. And it is this

---

22. Flavel, *Works*, 3:47.
23. Flavel, *Works*, 1:193.
24. Flavel, *Works*, 1:194.
25. Flavel, *Works*, 1:195.
26. Flavel, *Works*, 2:284.

knowledge of Christ that nurtures that "cheerfulness of heart" so prevalent in Flavel's writings. In the present volume, he shares his meditations on this glorious subject. He encourages us to cultivate a "sensible" and "practical" knowledge of Christ—that is, a knowledge that has its "seat in the heart."[27] He explains, "A saving, though an unmethodical knowledge of Christ, will bring us to heaven (John 17:2), but a regular and methodical, as well as a saving, knowledge of Him will bring heaven into us (Col. 2:2–3)."[28] With that in mind, I encourage you to read Flavel's work methodically (i.e., prayerfully and expectantly), keeping in mind his pastoral counsel from centuries ago: "To your work, Christian, to your work…. Whatever communion God and the soul maintains, it is in this way. Count all, therefore, but dross in comparison to that excellency which is the knowledge of Jesus Christ."[29]

—J. Stephen Yuille
Cambridge, Ontario
June 2020

---

27. Flavel, *Works*, 1:131.
28. Flavel, *Works*, 1:21.
29. Flavel, *Works*, 1:42.

# Christ's Humiliation

*And being found in fashion as a man, he humbled himself, and became obedient unto death, even the death of the cross.*
—PHILIPPIANS 2:8

We have considered how Christ was invested with the offices of prophet, priest, and king for the carrying out of the blessed design of our redemption.[1] The execution of these offices required that He should be deeply abased and highly exalted. He cannot, as our priest, offer Himself as a sacrifice to God unless He is humbled. He cannot, as our king, powerfully apply the virtue of His sacrifice unless He is exalted. If He had not stooped to the low estate of a man, He would not (as a priest) have had a sacrifice to offer, He would not (as a prophet) have been fit to teach us the will of God, and He would not (as a king) have been a suitable head to the church. And if He had not been exalted, His sacrifice could not have been carried within the veil before the Lord; His discoveries

---

1. See *Christ and His Threefold Office* (Grand Rapids: Reformation Heritage Books, 2021).

of God could not have been universal, effectual, and abiding; and His government could not have secured, protected, and defended the subjects of His kingdom.

He who intends to build high must lay the foundation low. Christ must have a distinct glory in heaven, transcending that of angels and humans. As He must be exalted infinitely above them, so He must first be humbled and abased below them.

Method requires that we first speak of Christ's state of humiliation. To that purpose, I have chosen this verse, which presents the Son under an almost total eclipse: "And being found in fashion as a man, he humbled himself, and became obedient unto death, even the death of the cross." He who was "beautiful and glorious" (Isa. 4:2), "the glory as of the only begotten of the Father" (John 1:14), "the brightness of his glory" (Heb. 1:3) was so veiled, clouded, and debased that He did not look like Himself. In reference to this humbled state, He declares, "I am a worm, and no man" (Ps. 22:6). In our verse, Christ's humiliation is described in three ways.

First, its *nature*: "he humbled himself." The word imports both a real and voluntary abasement. (1) It was real. He did not merely impersonate a humbled man. As man, He was really humbled. As God, He was humbled in respect of His majestic glory. (2) It was voluntary. It is not said that He was humbled, but that He humbled Himself. He was willing to stoop to this low state for us. And, indeed, the voluntary nature of His humiliation made it most acceptable to God, and it commends His love to us.

Second, its *degree*: He "became obedient unto death, even the death of the cross." Here we see the depth of Christ's humiliation. Not only did He become a man, but He died.

Not only did He die, but He did so hanging on a tree and dying the death of a malefactor.

Third, its *duration*: it continued from the first moment of His incarnation to the very moment of His vivification in the grave. So its terms are fixed here by the apostle: from the time He was "found in fashion as a man" (that is, from His incarnation) until His death on the cross, which also includes His time in the grave. This is how long His humiliation lasted.

*Doctrine: Christ's incarnation was marked by deep abasement and humiliation.*

We are now entering upon Christ's state of humiliation, which I will consider under three heads: His incarnation, His life, and His death. In this sermon, I will explain Christ's humiliation in His incarnation: He was "found in fashion as a man." We should not understand this to mean that He assumed a body as an assisting form, to appear temporarily in it. He was not an apparition in the shape of a man. Rather, He truly and really assumed our nature.

First, Christ was humbled by His incarnation because He who is "over all, God blessed for ever" (Rom. 9:5) was thereby brought into the rank and order of creatures. God "was manifest in the flesh" (1 Tim. 3:16). The eternal God is truly and properly called "the man Christ Jesus" (1 Tim. 2:5). It is a great wonder that God should dwell in a body of flesh (John 1:14), that the eternal God should be born in time, that the Ancient of Days should be as an infant of days. For the infinitely glorious Creator of all things to become a creature is a mystery exceeding all human understanding. The distance between God and the highest order of creatures is infinite. He is said to humble Himself to behold the things that are done in heaven. What a humiliation to behold the things in the lower world and to be born into it!

Second, Christ was humbled by His incarnation because He became not only a creature but an inferior creature. As man is nothing to God, so he is much inferior to the angels, so much below them that he is not able to bear the sight of an angel (Judg. 13:22). When the psalmist had contemplated the heavens, and viewed the celestial bodies which God had made, he cries out, "What is man, that thou art mindful of him? and the son of man, that thou visitest him?" (Ps. 8:4). When man was created, he was pure and perfect, and yet he was inferior to the angels. But Christ chooses this inferior order of creature and passes by the angelic nature. "For verily he took not on him the nature of angels; but he took on him the seed of Abraham" (Heb. 2:16).

Third, Christ was humbled by His incarnation because He assumed the human nature after sin had blotted its original glory and withered away its beauty and excellency. He did not come in our nature before the fall, while its glory was still in it. He came "in the likeness of sinful flesh" (Rom. 8:3)—that is, flesh that bore the miserable marks and effects of sin. Christ did not assume sinful flesh, or flesh really defiled by sin, for by the power of the Most High the body of Christ was so sanctified that no spot of original pollution remained in it. Though it did not have inherent uncleanness in it, it did have the effects of sin upon it. It was attended with human infirmities such as hunger, thirst, weariness, pain, mortality, and all the natural evils and weaknesses that clog our miserable natures and make them groan from day to day. Christ had to assume these sinless infirmities with the human nature because His bearing them was a part of His humiliation and part of His satisfaction for us. Moreover, it qualified Him as our high priest, filling Him with tender compassion for us.

Fourth, Christ was humbled by His incarnation because it so clouded His glory that He looked like a poor, sorry, and contemptible sinner in the eyes of the world. They scorned Him (Matt. 26:61). He "made himself of no reputation" (Phil. 2:7). It blotted His honor and reputation; as a result, He lost all esteem and honor from those who saw Him (Matt. 13:55). He looked like a poor man, traveling up and down the country in hunger, thirst, and weariness. Who would ever have thought that He was the Creator of the world, the Prince of the kings of the earth? Is not this astonishing self-denial? He who was adored by all creation became a footstool for every rebel to tread upon.

Fifth, Christ was humbled by His incarnation because it distanced Him from His Father and the ineffable joy and pleasure that He enjoyed eternally with Him. He enjoyed a high rate of communion with God while He walked here in the flesh. But to live by faith (as Christ did on earth) is one thing, and to be in the bosom of God (as He was before His incarnation) is another. To have the ineffable delights of God perpetuated and continued to Him without one moment's interruption in eternity is one thing, and to have His soul filled at times with the joy of the Lord is another. He was reduced to such a low ebb of spiritual comforts as to be forced to cry, "My God, my God, why hast thou forsaken me?" (Ps. 22:1).

**Application**

*Lesson 1*

We infer the fullness and completeness of Christ's satisfaction as the sweet firstfruits of His incarnation. We offended and violated God's law, but God Himself became man to repair the breach and satisfy for the wrong committed. The greater Christ was, the greater was His humiliation. And the greater His humiliation, the more full and complete was His satisfaction. And the more complete Christ's satisfaction, the more certain is the believer's consolation. If He had not stooped so low, our joy and comfort could not be exalted so high. The depth of the foundation is the strength of the superstructure.

*Lesson 2*

We have a tremendous pattern of self-denial in Christ's example (John 13:14). He became a worm, reproach, and curse. Do the least slights and neglects rankle our hearts and poison them with discontent, malice, and revenge? Our Savior was meek and lowly. He looked not at His own things, but ours (Phil. 2:4). Does it become us to be proud and selfish?

*Lesson 3*

Those who perish under the gospel perish without excuse. Christ laid aside His robes of majesty and glory, put on our garments of flesh, came down from His throne, and brought salvation to us. Surely, the lower Christ stooped to save us, the lower we will sink under wrath if we neglect so great a salvation. Christ is brought low, but unbelievers will lay Him yet lower, even under their feet. They will tread the Son of God under foot (Heb. 10:29). O poor sinners, your damnation is just if you refuse grace brought home by Christ Himself to your very doors! The Lord grant that this is not your case!

## Lesson 4

No one can love like Christ, for His love to us is matchless. Its strength, liberty, and immutability put a luster on it, beyond all examples. Surely, it was a strong love indeed that made Him lay aside His glory, to be found in fashion as a man, for our salvation. His love, like Himself, is wonderful.

## Lesson 5

We should exalt and honor the One who was so abused for our sakes. First, we should speak frequently and delightfully of Christ. We have every reason to exalt the author of our salvation, who has freed us from a dreadful bondage. We who have escaped the eternal wrath of God by the humiliation of the Son of God ought to extol our great Redeemer and forever celebrate His praises.

Second, we should trust in Christ for whatever is still unfulfilled in the promises. Unbelief usually argues from one of these two grounds: Can God do this? or Will God do this? It is questioning either His power or His will. But His power to save should never be questioned by anyone who knows what infinite burdens and sufferings Christ supported in our nature. Surely, His willingness to save should never be questioned by anyone who considers how low He was content to stoop for us.

Third, we should draw near to God "through the veil, that is to say, his flesh" (Heb. 10:20). God has made Christ's flesh a veil between the brightness of His glory and us. It serves to rebate the unsupportable glory and to give admission to it. Through this body of flesh are all outlets of grace from God to us, and all returns to God again. It is made the great medium of our communion with God.

Fourth, we should apply ourselves to Him in all wants, troubles, and temptations, as to One who is tenderly sensible of our case and most willing to relieve us. This was one of the inducements that persuaded and invited Him to take our nature, that He might be furnished abundantly with tender compassion for us, from the sense He should have of our infirmities in His own body (Heb. 2:17). By being in our nature, Christ knows experimentally what our wants, fears, temptations, and distresses are, and so He is able to have compassion. O may our hearts work upon this admirable condescension of Christ, until they are filled with it, and our lips say, "Thanks be to God for Jesus Christ!"

# 2

# A Humble Life

*And being found in fashion as a man, he humbled himself, and became obedient unto death, even the death of the cross.*
—PHILIPPIANS 2:8

We considered the meaning of this verse in the previous sermon. But it can never be considered enough, for it holds forth Christ's humbled state during the time of His abode on earth. Christ's humiliation was proposed to you under these three general heads: (1) His humiliation in His incarnation, (2) His humiliation in His life, and (3) His humiliation in His death. In the last sermon, I explained how He was humbled by His incarnation. I will now explain how He was humbled in His life.

*Doctrine: Christ's life was marked by deep debasement and humiliation.*

The Scriptures include very little about Christ's private life, and it is not my design to expound the passages that the evangelists have preserved for us. I will consider the more observable degrees by which He was especially humbled.

## Christ's Circumcision

Christ was humbled by His very infancy—by His circumcision according to the law. Being an Israelite, He submitted to the Old Testament ceremonies and ordinances (Luke 2:21). In so doing, He was greatly humbled in these two respects.

First, Christ obligated Himself to keep the whole law, though He was the lawmaker. "For I testify again to every man that is circumcised, that he is a debtor to do the whole law" (Gal. 5:3). The apostle means that those who are bound to keep one part of the ceremonial law do thereby bind themselves to keep it all, and those who are debtors in duty to keep the whole law quickly become debtors in regard of penalty. Christ, therefore, becomes our surety to pay both those debts: the debt of duty and the debt of penalty. By His circumcision, He commits Himself to pay the whole debt of duty by fulfilling all righteousness. Though His obedience was so exact and perfect that He contracted no debt of penalty for any transgression of His own, He obligates Himself to pay the debt of penalty (which He had contracted) by suffering all the pains due to transgressors. It was no small measure for Christ to bind Himself to the law as a subject made under it, for He was the lawgiver and above all law. In this way the sovereignty of God was veiled and obscured by His subjection.

Second, Christ represented Himself to the world, not only as a subject but as a sinner. When this ordinance (i.e., circumcision) passed upon Him, it seemed to imply that corruption was indeed in Him. Circumcision served to remind

Abraham and his seed of the corruption of their hearts (Jer. 4:4). Hence, the rebellious and unmortified are called "stiff-necked and uncircumcised in heart" (Acts 7:51). As it served to convince of natural uncleanness, so it signified the "putting off the body of the sins of the flesh" (Col. 2:11). Therefore, by submitting to this institution, Christ veiled His sovereignty. He was also represented as a sinner to the world, though He was most pure and holy in Himself.

### Christ's Persecution

Christ was humbled by persecution. He was banished almost as soon as He was born (Matt. 2:13). Psalm 22 contains a detailed description of Christ's suffering. "For dogs have compassed me: the assembly of the wicked have inclosed me" (v. 16). Christ was not only killed but hunted to be killed. This hunt began the moment He was born. How great a humiliation is this to the Son of God! Not only did He become an infant, but even in His infancy He was driven out of His own land as a vagabond.

### Christ's Poverty

Christ was humbled by poverty. He lived as a poor man all His days (2 Cor. 8:9). He never owned a house, but lived in other men's houses. His outward condition was more destitute than that of the birds of the air or beasts of the earth (Matt. 8:20). Sometimes He was hungry and had nothing to eat (Mark 11:12). As for money, he had none (Matt. 17:27). Christ did not come to be served, but to serve (Matt. 20:28). He did not come to amass earthly treasures but to bestow heavenly ones. He did not give a thought to those things that consume thousands of our thoughts. Indeed, He came to be humbled and to teach us by His example of the vanity of this world. Therefore, He went before us in a chosen and voluntary poverty.

### Christ's Temptation

Christ was humbled by Satan's horrid temptations (Luke 4:1–14). Could there be anything more burdensome to Him, who delighted in His Father from all eternity, than to be found in the wilderness with the devil and face such horrid blasphemy? How great a humiliation must it be to the great God, to be humbled to this! To see a slave setting himself over his master! Surely, this was a deep abasement to the Son of God.

### Christ's Compassion

Christ was humbled by His sympathy with others under all the burdens that made Him groan. His heart was so tender that every groan for sin, or under the effects of sin, pierced Him. "[He] himself took our infirmities, and bare our sicknesses" (Matt. 8:16–17). It is said that when He saw Mary weeping, He "groaned in the spirit" (John 11:33). Christ's heart flowed with pity for those who did not have one drop of pity for themselves (Luke 19:41–42). He mourned for those who would not mourn for their own sins (Mark 3:5). This was one of those things that made Him "a man of sorrows, and acquainted with grief" (Isa. 53:3). The more holy a person is, the more he is grieved and afflicted by others' sin. The more tender a person is, the more he is pierced by seeing the miseries that lie upon others. It is certain that there has never been a more holy, tender, sensible, and compassionate heart than Christ's.

**Christ's Reception**

Christ was humbled by the ungrateful and unworthy manner in which the world received Him. He was not treated like a savior, but as the vilest of men. He came from heaven "to give his life a ransom for many" (Matt. 20:28). He was not sent "to condemn the world; but that the world through him might be saved" (John 3:17). He came to "destroy the works of the devil" (1 John 3:8). He came to "proclaim liberty to the captives" (Isa. 61:1). How should the world have welcomed Him? What acclamations of joy and demonstrations of gratitude should He have received! Instead, they hated Him (John 15:18) and despised Him (Matt. 13:55). They accused Him of working His miracles by the power of the devil (Matt. 12:24). They trod upon Him as a worm (Ps. 22:6). They struck Him on the head and spat in His face (Matt. 27:29–32). All this was a great abasement to the Son of God. He "endured such contradiction of sinners against himself" (Heb. 12:3).

**Application**

*Lesson 1*

From the first degree of Christ's humiliation, we infer that justice may set both hand and seal to the acquittance and discharge of believers. Christ committed Himself to be the law's paymaster—to pay its utmost demand and to bear the yoke of obedience that no one before Him could bear. As His circumcision obligated Him to keep the whole law, so He was most precise and punctual in the observance of it. He was so exact that the sharp eye of divine justice could spy the least flaw in it, but acknowledged full payment, and stood ready to sign the believer a full acquittance (Rom. 3:25). If Christ had not been thus obligated, we would never have been discharged. If His obedience had not been an entire, complete, and perfect thing, our justification would never have been so.

## Lesson 2

From the second degree, we infer that the greatest innocence is not exempt from injury and persecution. Who is more innocent than Christ? And who has been more persecuted? Persecution follows piety (John 17:14; 2 Tim. 3:12). Whoever resolves to live holy must never expect to live quietly. All who will live godly will exert holiness in their lives. This troubles the conscience of the ungodly. It is this that enrages them, for there is an enmity and antipathy between them and godliness (Gal. 4:29). But it must be so to conform us to Christ. He suffered meekly and quietly. To do well and suffer ill is Christlike.

## Lesson 3

From the third degree, we infer that those who are full of grace and holiness may be destitute of earthly comforts. There was an overflowing fullness of grace in Christ, and yet He was often without outward comforts. This is how it has fared with many of God's people (1 Cor. 4:11). We must remember that when wants pinch hard, these are not marks of God's displeasure with us. He has dealt no worse with us than He did with His own Son. We must also remember we are on our way to a plentiful country, where all our wants will be supplied (James 2:5). The meanness of our present condition will add to the luster of our future condition.

*Lesson 4*

From the fourth degree, we infer that those in whom Satan has no interest may have most trouble from him in this world. "The prince of this world cometh, and hath nothing in me" (John 14:30). If he cannot be a conqueror, he will seek to be a troubler. It was the love and wisdom of Christ that allowed the devil to try all his darts upon Him, so that by this experience He might be filled with pity to assist those who are tempted. As he set on Christ, so much more will he set upon us. Sometimes he shoots the fiery darts of blasphemous injections. These fall as flashes of lightning on the dry grass that instantly sets all ablaze. It is accompanied with a thunderclap of inward horror that strikes the very heart and shakes all into confusion within.

Various rules are prescribed in this case to relieve poor distressed souls. The best rule is this: "Above all, taking the shield of faith, wherewith ye shall be able to quench all the fiery darts of the wicked" (Eph. 6:16). We must set our faith on our Savior, who passed through temptations before us, and particularly consider three things: (1) the variety of temptations that befell Christ, (2) the victory of Christ over all those temptations, and (3) the benefits of His victory for us (Heb. 2:18).

Some people object to the notion that Christ was tempted like us (Heb. 4:15), because there is a vast difference between His temptations and our temptations. Simply put, the devil found nothing in Him (John 14:30). Christ was never internally defiled, though externally assaulted, but we are defiled as well as troubled. The solution is to remember that if Christ had been internally defiled, He could not have been a fit mediator for us, nor could we have had any benefit from His temptations or sufferings for us. Being tempted, and being free from the defilement of sin, He has not only made satisfaction for our sins but He has gained an experimental sense of the misery of our condition.

*Lesson 5*

From the fifth degree, we infer that a compassionate spirit toward those who labor under burdens of sin or affliction is Christlike and truly excellent (Rom. 12:15; 2 Cor. 11:29; Col. 3:12). Three things promote sympathy in Christians: (1) Christ's pity for us (Isa. 63:9), (2) our relationship to God's afflicted people (1 Cor. 12:25), and (3) our awareness that we might soon need from others what others now need from us (Gal. 6:1).

*Lesson 6*

From the sixth degree, we infer that the world's judgment of people and their worth is not to be regarded (Heb. 11:38). Where it fixes its marks of hatred, we may usually find that which invites our love and respect. It should not trouble us to be under the insults and affronts of a blind world. We must labor to stand right in the judgment of God and not trouble ourselves on account of unbelievers' rash censures. From the whole of Christ's humiliation in His life, we learn to pass through all the troubles of life with a contented and composed spirit. Christ, our forerunner, was persecuted but bore it meekly; He was poor but never murmured; He was tempted but never yielded to temptation. When, therefore, we pass through any of these trials, we can look to Christ. He managed Himself in similar circumstances, not only to set an example for us but to leave behind a blessing for those who follow in His footsteps.

# 3

# A Prayer of Commendation

*And now I am no more in the world, but these are in the world, and I come to thee. Holy Father, keep through thine own name those whom thou hast given me, that they may be one, as we are.*
—JOHN 17:11

We come to the last step in Christ's humiliation: His death on the cross. There were six acts of preparation: three on His part and three on His enemies' part. His preparations included (1) His commendation of His friends to His Father, (2) His institution of a commemorative sign to refresh the memory of His death in the hearts of His people, and (3) His pouring out of His soul to God by prayer in the garden.

Our verse contains the first of these. Christ sets His house in order and prays for His people. His love was always tender toward them, but its greatest manifestation was at His departure. He manifested it in two ways: (1) in leaving them with grounds of comfort in His heavenly sermon (John 14–16) and (2) in pouring out His soul to the Father for them in His heavenly prayer (John 17). In this prayer, Christ gives them a sample of His glorious work of intercession, which He was going to perform in heaven for them. His heart overflowed, for He was about to leave them. The last words of a dying man are remarkable. How much more the last words of a dying savior!

Here we have Christ's petitions (or requests) on behalf of His people. The sum of them all is that His Father would keep them through His name. The term *keep* implies danger. And there is a double danger implied in this request: danger in respect of sin and danger in respect of ruin and destruction. The means of preservation from both is the name (i.e., the power) of God (Prov. 18:10). It is not our strength or wisdom that keeps us, but God's mighty power. This protecting power, however, does not exclude our care and diligence. "[Ye] are kept by the power of God through faith unto salvation" (1 Peter 1:5). God keeps His people, and yet we are to keep ourselves in God's love (Jude 21). This is the sum of the petition.

Christ presses His request with arguments drawn from His condition ("I am no more in the world"), their condition ("but these are in the world"), and the joint interest that He and His Father have in them ("those whom thou hast given me").

*Doctrine: Christ's fatherly care and tender love was eminently manifested in the pleading prayer He poured out for His people at His departing from them.*

When Christ comes to die, He blesses His children. Here we discover His dear and tender love for them (John 13:1). His last act in this world was an act of blessing (Luke 24:50–51).

**The Mercies**
We will begin by considering the mercies that Christ requested for His people. First, He requested their preservation from

sin and danger: "keep through thine own name those whom thou hast given me." This is explained in verse 15, "I pray not that thou shouldest take them out of the world, but that thou shouldest keep them from the evil." This is why we are preserved amid a world of temptations. This is why we are not ruined and destroyed amid multitudes of malicious enemies who are set on fire by hell. The sin that is in us, and the malice that is in others, would quickly ruin our souls and bodies if it were not for God's hand that keeps us every moment.

Second, Christ requested the blessing of union among His people: "that they may be one, as we are." This union is not only a choice mercy in itself but a special means of accomplishing our preservation. Their union with one another is a special means to preserve them all.

Third, Christ requested that His joy might be fulfilled in them (v. 13). He desired to provide for their joy, even when the hour of His greatest sorrow was at hand. It is as if He had said, "O, My Father, I am to leave these dear ones in a world of troubles and perplexities. I know their hearts will be subject to frequent despondencies. O let Me obtain the delights of divine joy for them before I go. I would not only have them live, but live joyfully."

Fourth, Christ requested that His people might be sanctified through the Word (v. 17). He wanted them to be more sanctified than they were at present, by a deeper implantation of gracious habits and principles in their hearts. This is an extraordinary mercy in itself—to have holiness spread itself throughout their souls. Nothing is in itself more desirable. And it is also a great help to their preservation, union, and joy, which are all advanced by increasing sanctification.

Fifth, Christ requested that they might be with Him to "behold [his] glory" (v. 24). This is the best and ultimate privilege. The end of His coming down from heaven, and returning there again, all runs into this—to bring many sons and daughters to glory. Christ requests no mere trifles, no small things for His people. Nothing but the best will suffice.

### The Arguments

As Christ makes His requests to His Father, He presents a number of arguments. The first is the common interest that He and His Father have in the people for whom He prays. "All mine are thine, and thine are mine" (v. 10). They are the Father's children as well as Christ's. The Father set His eternal love upon them, and in that love He gave them to Christ. Everyone cares for his own. These are the Father's own; therefore, He will save, keep, comfort, and sanctify them.

The second argument is Christ's honor. "And I am glorified in them" (v. 10). The Father's heart is entirely set upon exalting and glorifying His Son. Christ's glory is tied to His people, meaning His active glory and praise must rise from them. If His people perish, then what will be left of Christ's active glory? Thus, He appeals to His glory in His prayer to the Father.

The third argument is Christ's departure. "And now I am no more in the world" (v. 11). This statement must not be taken simply and universally, as if Christ is no longer (in any sense) in this world. It must be taken respectively, as to His corporeal presence. He was removed physically from His people. He leaves His poor children with sadness and trouble. While He was with them, He was a sweet relief to their souls, whatever troubles they encountered. They had His counsels to direct them, His reproofs to correct them, and His comforts to support them. The very sight of Him was an unspeakable joy and refreshment to their souls. But now He is leaving. All the comfort and benefit they had from His presence is cut off. What will become of them once He is gone? And so Christ asks His Father to look after them.

The fourth argument is their danger. "But these are in the world" (v. 11). The world is a sinful and infecting place. It lies in wickedness. It is a hard thing for poor, weak, and imperfect people to escape its pollutions. If we do, we cannot escape its troubles, persecutions, and oppositions. We are like children in a foreign country, soldiers in an enemy's camp, sheep among wolves, or treasure among thieves. Since Christ must leave His people in the midst of a sinful, troublesome, and dangerous world, He asks His Father to look after them, provide for them, and take special care of them.

The fifth argument is Christ's ascension. "And I come to thee" (v. 11). The beloved Son, in whom the Father delights, is coming home. He takes every step of the way in blood and suffering. The purpose of His coming to the Father is for them. He comes to heaven in the capacity of an advocate, to plead for them. He comes to His Father and their Father, His God and their God. He knows the Father will not deny Him.

The sixth argument is Christ's faithfulness. "While I was with them in the world, I kept them in thy name: those that thou gavest me I have kept, and none of them is lost, but the son of perdition" (v. 12). The Father committed to Christ a certain number of elect, to be redeemed by Him. He undertook the responsibility, and He has been faithful. He redeemed them, preserved them, and confirmed them. Now He commits them to the Father's care. Not one was lost, except the son of perdition, whom the Father never gave to the Son.

### The Reasons

Why did Christ pray and plead in this way with the Father when He was about to die? It was not because the Father was unwilling to grant His requests. Christ did not wrestle the Father's mercies out of an unwilling hand, for He tells us, "The Father himself loveth you" (John 16:27). The Father does good of His own accord. The reasons for Christ's prayer are as follows.

First, Christ foresaw a great trial at hand. He knew how much His people would be sifted in the coming hour. He knew the power of darkness was drawing near. He knew their faith would be greatly shaken when they saw their Shepherd smitten and the sheep scattered. He foresaw the difficulties His poor people would face, between a busy devil and a bad heart. Therefore, He prays and pleads with such fervor for them.

Second, Christ wanted to give an example of His intercessory work in heaven so that His people would understand what He is now doing for them in heaven. This was His last prayer on earth, and it shows us what affections and dispositions He carried with Him. It shows us that He who was so earnest with God on our behalf will not forget us in the other world. His intercession in heaven is carried much higher than this. It is performed in a way more suitable to that state of honor to which He is now exalted. Here He used cries, tears, and prostrations of body in His prayers. But there His intercession is carried on in a more majestic way, becoming an exalted Christ.

Third, Christ wanted to leave this prayer as a standing monument of His fatherlike care and love for His people to the end of the world. This is why He delivered the prayer so publicly, not withdrawing from the disciples to be alone with God. He delivered it in their presence: "these things I speak in the world" (John 17:13). Not only was it publicly delivered, but it was by providence recorded by John, so that it might stand to all generations as a testimony of Christ's tender care and love for His people.

### The Evidences

If you ask how this demonstrates Christ's tender care and love for His people, I answer with these two particulars. First, Christ's love was manifested in the mercies He chose for His people. He does not pray for health, honor, riches, and so on, but for preservation from sin, joy in God, sanctification, and eternal glory. He will not be satisfied with anything but the best mercies. He will settle these as a heritage upon His children. O see the love of Christ! When we look over our spiritual inheritance in Christ, and compare it with the richest, fairest, sweetest inheritances on earth, we see what poor things these really are. O the love of a tender savior!

Second, Christ's love was manifested in the way He so affectionately pleaded our concerns with God, even when a world of sorrow encompassed Him. A cup of wrath was about to be delivered into His hand. All His cares and thoughts should have been employed on His own account, to mind His own sufferings, and yet He does (as it were) forget His own sorrows, to mind our peace and comfort. O love unspeakable!

## Application

*Lesson 1*

The perseverance of the saints is unquestionable. Do we hear how Christ pleads, uses His arguments, chooses His words, and winds up His spirit to the highest pitch of zeal and fervency? And can we doubt success? Can the Father deny the pleading of such a Son? Christ has the art and skill of prevailing with God. He has the tongue of the learned. The Father loves us and is inclined to do us good; therefore, who can doubt of Christ's success? Christ's cause in heaven for us is just and righteous, and the manner in which He pleads is powerful; therefore, His success is unquestionable.

If Christ pleads the cause of His people with the Father, and uses His oratory with Him, there is no doubt of His prevailing. Every word in this prayer is a chosen arrow, drawn by a strong and skillful hand. We do not need to question if it hits the mark. He prays, "Father, keep through thine own name those whom thou hast given me" (John 17:11). Surely, they will be kept. When dangers surround us, when fears and doubts multiply within, we should think of the encouragement Christ gave to Peter: "I have prayed for thee" (Luke 22:32).

*Lesson 2*

Christ has great esteem for believers. "I come to thee. Holy Father, keep through thine own name those whom thou hast given me." Surely, believers are dear to Christ, and for good reason, for He has paid dearly for them. They are a peculiar treasure to Him, above all the people on earth (Ex. 19:5). O how precious should Christ be to us! We were first and last upon His heart. He prayed for us. He wrestled with God for us when the sorrows of death encompassed Him. How much are we engaged, not only to love Him and esteem Him but to be in pangs of love for Him when we feel the pangs of death upon us! The very last whisper of our departing soul should be this: "Blessed be God for Jesus Christ!"

# 4

# A Commemorative Sign

*The Lord Jesus the same night in which he was betrayed took bread: And when he had given thanks, he brake it, and said, Take, eat; this is my body, which is broken for you: this do in remembrance of me. After the same manner also he took the cup, when he had supped, saying, This cup is the new testament in my blood: this do ye, as oft as ye drink it, in remembrance of me.*
—1 CORINTHIANS 11:23–25

Having recommended His dear charge to the Father, Christ institutes His last supper to be the memorial of His death until His second coming. In so doing, He graciously provides for the comfort of His people. This was Christ's second act of preparation, and it manifests no less love than the first. The apostle notes four things in these verses.

First, the *author* of this ordinance: "the Lord Jesus." It is an effect of His lordly power and kingly authority (Matt. 28:18). The government is upon His shoulders (Isa. 9:6). He shall bear the glory (Zech. 6:13). He came out of the bosom of the Father, and is acquainted with all the counsels that are there, and thus He knows what is acceptable to God. He alone can give creatures, by His blessing, their sacramental virtue and efficacy. Bread and wine are naturally fit to refresh and nourish our bodies, but what fitness have they to nourish souls? Surely none but what they receive from Christ's blessing.

Second, the *time* of this ordinance: "the same night in which he was betrayed." It could not have been sooner, because the Passover must first be celebrated. It could not have been later, for that night He was arrested. It is, therefore, emphatically expressed, "the same night." By instituting it "the same night," He gives abundant evidence of His care for His people by spending so much of the time He had left on their account.

Third, the *content* of this ordinance: bread and wine. These signs represent glorious mysteries—namely, Christ crucified and the proper nourishment of believers. Bread and wine shadow forth the flesh and blood of the crucified Christ. Their usefulness is very great: bread maintains natural life, while wine cheers the heart. The corn must be ground in the mill and the grapes must be squeezed in the winepress before we can have bread or wine. When all this is done, they must be received into the body to nourish it. The preciousness of these elements is not so much from their own natures, as their use and end. As lively signs, they shadow forth a crucified Christ and represent Him to us in His red garments.

Fourth, the *design* of this ordinance: "in remembrance of me." Christ knew how inclined our base hearts would be to forget Him and how detrimental this would be to us. Therefore, He appoints a sign to be remembered.

*Doctrine: Christ's sacramental memorial is a special mark of His care and love for His people.*

O what manner of love is this! The bread and wine are marks of love and honor. As often as we look upon this portrait of Christ, we should remember that He endured for our sakes. These are the wounds He received for us. These are the marks of that love which surpasses the love of creatures.

**How We Remember**

Remembrance is the return of the mind to an object with which it was formerly conversant. It returns in one of two ways. The first is a *speculative* remembrance. This is to call to mind the history of Christ and His sufferings. The second is an *affective* remembrance. This occurs when we call Christ and His death to our minds to such a degree that we feel powerful impressions upon our hearts. "Peter remembered the word of Jesus…. And he went out, and wept bitterly" (Matt. 26:75). His heart was melted by his remembrance. Such a remembrance of Christ is that which is here intended. It is indeed a gracious remembrance of Christ.

A speculative remembrance has no grace in it. The time will come when Judas, and the Jews who betrayed Christ, will remember *speculatively* what they did. They will "wail because of him" (Rev. 1:7). Judas will remember that he betrayed Christ. Pilate will remember that he sentenced Christ to death. The soldiers will remember that they crowned Christ with thorns. But this remembrance will be their torment, not their benefit.

The remembrance, intended in this verse, is not a bare historical and speculative remembrance, but a gracious and affective remembrance. It includes the following. (1) A saving knowledge of Christ. We cannot remember what we never knew, nor remember savingly what we never knew savingly. There have been many previous dealings between Christ and His people. At the Lord's Supper, their acquaintance is renewed, and the remembrance of His love and goodness is refreshed and revived (Song 1:4). (2) A discerning of Christ at the sacrament. Without this, there is no remembrance of Him. When the eye of faith has seen Christ, it calls up the affections, saying, "Come see the Lord! These are the wounds He received for me. This is the One who loved me and gave Himself for me. This is His flesh and His blood. His arms were stretched out upon the cross to embrace me. His head hung down to kiss me. Come, all powers and affections of my soul! Come, see the Lord!" (3) A stirring of the affections. This suitable impression made upon the affections is the nature of that precious thing we call communion with God.

Various representations of Christ are made at His table. (1) We call to mind the infinite wisdom of God who contrived and established the glorious and mysterious design of redemption. The effect of this is wonder and admiration (Eph. 3:10). (2) We call to mind the severity of God. O how severe is the justice of God! There was no abatement, no mercy, for His own Son. This makes a double impression on the heart. First, it causes just and deep indignation against sin. When we remember that sin put Christ to all that shame and disgrace, and that He was wounded for our transgressions, we are filled with hatred of sin. Second, it produces a humble adoration of the goodness and mercy of God. "Lord, if Your wrath had seized on me as it did on Christ, what would have happened to me?" (3) We call to mind the love of Christ. He assumed a body and soul, to bear the wrath of God for our sins. When that surpassing love breaks out in its glory upon us, we are transported and ravished with it. What manner of love is this! Here is a love large enough to encompass the heavens. (4) We call to mind the fruit of Christ's death: His satisfaction for sin and His purchase of an eternal inheritance. This begets thankfulness and confidence in us. Christ is dead, and His death has made satisfaction for our sin. Christ is dead; therefore, we will never die. Who will separate us from the love of God?

What is there in the sacrament that leads us to remember Christ? As a memorial, it serves as a pledge (or token) of Christ's love. As a sign, it signifies His suffering for us and our union with Him. The breaking of the bread and pouring of the wine signify the former, while our eating and drinking points to the latter. This ordinance has an excellent use for the affectionate remembrance of Christ because it is an instructive sign. It teaches us that Christ is the bread on which our souls live. It also teaches us that the New Testament is now in its full force, and no substantial alteration can be made to it, since the testator is dead, and by His death He has ratified it (Heb. 9:16–17).

### What We Remember

In the sacrament, Christ has left a special mark of His love for His people. How? First, it confirms His people's faith to the end of the world. As an evident proof that the New Testament is in full force, it tends as much to our satisfaction as the legal execution of a deed. When He says, "Take, eat," it is as if God were standing before us at the table with Christ and all the promises were in His hand. Does not this promote and confirm our faith?

Second, it enlarges His people's joy and comfort. Do we so prize, esteem, and value Him that nothing but His love will satisfy us? If so, we know that He is ours. We can take our Christ into the arms of our faith this day. Does not this create in us a joy that transcends all the joys and pleasures in this world?

Third, it encourages His people's mortification of their corruption. Nothing tends more to the killing of sin than this. Christ's blood, as it is food to our faith, so it is poison to our lusts. When we see in the sacrament Christ's suffering for our sin, how can we live in it any longer?

Fourth, it excites His people's love into a lively flame. How does the soul (if I may so speak) passionately love Christ at such a time? What has He done, what has He suffered for me! What great things has my Jesus given, and what great things has He forgiven! Here the soul is melted by love at His feet. It is pained with love.

Fifth, it is one of the strongest bonds of union between Christ and His people (1 Cor. 10:17). Here we are sealed up to the same inheritance, our corruptions are slain, our love to Christ and consequently to each other is improved. It is certainly one of the strongest ties in the world to wrap up gracious hearts in a bundle of love.

### Application

*Lesson 1*

Despite all that Christ has done, suffered, and promised, we are apt to forget Him. He should never be absent from our thoughts and affections. We should carry Him in our desires and delights; we should be filled with longing thoughts toward Him; we should lie down at night with Him in our thoughts; and our dreams should be filled with sweet visions of Him. But, O, the baseness of our hearts! We live in a world of sensible objects that rob us of Christ.

Though Christ is in the highest glory in heaven, He does not forget us. He has engraved us on the palms of His hands. He thinks of us, when we forget Him. All the honor of angels in heaven cannot divert His thoughts from us for one moment, but every trifle that meets us in the way is enough to divert our thoughts from Him. Why do we not loathe ourselves for this? Is it a pain or burden to carry Christ in our thoughts in the world? Will such thoughts thrust Christ out of our minds? For shame! Nothing but Christ takes up the thoughts of the saints in heaven, yet they are never satiated. O we must learn to live nearer that heavenly life! We must never cease praying and striving until we can say, "My soul shall be satisfied as with marrow and fatness; and my mouth shall praise thee with joyful lips: When I remember thee upon my bed, and meditate on thee in the night watches" (Ps. 63:5–6).

*Lesson 2*
The celebration of the sacrament is a heartmelting season because it is the most affecting representation of Christ. As the gospel offers Christ to the ear in the most sweet and affecting sounds of grace, so the sacrament offers Him to the eye in the most pleasing visions that are on this side of heaven.

At the sacrament, our hearts can pour out floods of tears (Zech. 12:10). I dare not affirm that everyone whose heart is broken by the believing sight of Christ will weep, but that they will be truly humbled for sin and seriously affected with Christ's grace. We need to distinguish between what is essential and what is contingent to spiritual sorrow. A deep displeasure with sin and a hearty resolution for its complete mortification are essential to all spiritual sorrow. Tears are accidental. If we have the former, we need not trouble ourselves for lack of the latter.

When we see who it is that our sins have pierced, how great, how glorious, how wonderful a person He is, who was so humbled and abased for such as us, it cannot but tenderly affect our hearts.

*Lesson 3*
The affective remembrance of Christ is of great advantage at all times to God's people, for it is the immediate end of one of the greatest ordinances that Christ appointed for the church. Frequent recognitions of Christ are useful to us for the following reasons. First, this is the best means for dissolving and quickening a dead and hard heart.

Second, this is the most powerful restraint for sin. "How shall we, that are dead to sin, live any longer therein?" (Rom. 6:2). We are crucified with Christ. What have we to do with sin? We should think about this when we are struggling with temptation. How can I do this and crucify the Son of God afresh? Has He not suffered enough already? Will I make Him groan (as it were) for me in heaven? No! I will have nothing to do with sin, for it cost infinite and precious blood to expiate it.

Third, this is a relieving and satisfying ordinance. The cup of the New Testament is Christ's blood shed for the remission of sins. "Who shall lay any thing to the charge of God's elect?… Who is he that condemneth? It is Christ that died" (Rom. 8:33–34).

Fourth, this is able to fortify us with courage and resolution when we stagger on account of our sufferings for Christ in this world. Did Christ face the wrath of men and the wrath of God too? Did He stand with steadfast patience and resolution under such troubles as no one has ever known? And will I shrink for a trifle? He did not serve me so. I will arm myself with the like mind (1 Peter 2:23).

Fifth, this will help us to believe in hope against hope. Does our faith stagger at the promises? Can we not rest upon a promise? This is God's seal added to His covenant, which binds fast all that He has spoken.

Sixth, this will cause us to redeem the time. Do we idle away precious time? What is more suited to cure us than the remembrance of Christ at the sacrament? When we consider that our time and talents are not our own, but Christ's, and when we consider that we are bought with a price (a great price indeed), we will see that we are strictly obliged to glorify God with our soul and body (2 Cor. 5:15). This will powerfully awaken a dull and lazy spirit.

In a word, what grace is there that this remembrance of Christ cannot quicken? What sin can it not mortify? What duty can it not animate? It is of great use in all cases to the people of God.

*Lesson 4*

This ordinance is able to preserve Christ's remembrance to the end of the world. His blood never dries up. The beauty of this rose of Sharon never withers. He is the same yesterday, today, and forever. As His body in the grave saw no corruption, so neither can His love, or any of His excellencies, see corruption. When we have set our eyes on Him in heaven for millions of years, He will be as fresh and beautiful as at the beginning. Other beauties have their prime, but Christ abides eternally. Our greatest delight in creatures is usually at first acquaintance. When we come near to them, and see more of them, the edge of our delight is abated. But the longer we know Christ, and the closer we come to Him, the more we will see of His glory. Every view of Christ entertains the mind with a fresh delight. He is (as it were) a new Christ every day, and yet still the same Christ. Blessed be God for Jesus Christ!

# 5

# Christ's Agony

*And he was withdrawn from them about a stone's cast,
and kneeled down, and prayed, saying, Father, if thou be
willing, remove this cup from me: nevertheless not my
will, but thine, be done. And there appeared an angel
unto him from heaven, strengthening him. And being in
an agony he prayed more earnestly: and his sweat was as
it were great drops of blood falling down to the ground.*
—LUKE 22:41–44

The hour has almost arrived. In a very little while, the Son
of Man will be betrayed into the hands of sinners. He has
affectionately commended His children to His Father. He
has set His house in order and ordained a memorial of His
death to be left with His people. There is but one more thing
to do before the tragedy begins: He must commend Himself
by prayer to the Father. Once this is done, He is ready. This
last act of Christ's preparation is contained in these verses, in
which we observe the following.

First, Christ's *prayer*: "he was withdrawn from them about
a stone's cast, and kneeled down, and prayed." He was in a posture of prayer when the enemy came. He was pleading with

God in prayer for strength to carry Him through this heavy trial. This prayer was remarkable for its solitude; He withdrew about a stone's throw, where only His Father could hear Him. It was remarkable for its intensity; He prayed with strong cries (Heb. 5:7). And it was remarkable for its humility; He fell to the ground, rolling (as it were) in the dust at His Father's feet.

Second, Christ's *agony*: "his sweat was as it were great drops of blood falling down to the ground." This is not stated by way of hyperbole or similitude. It was a real bloody sweat.

Third, Christ's *relief*: "there appeared an angel unto him from heaven, strengthening him." The Lord of angels needed the comfort of an angel. It was time to have a little refreshment when His face and body stood as full of drops of blood as the drops of dew on the grass.

*Doctrine: Christ was praying to His Father in an extraordinary agony when they came to arrest Him in the garden.*

### The Place of Christ's Prayer

It was in the garden of Gethsemane. This garden was located very close to the city of Jerusalem. The city had twelve gates, five of which were on the east side. The most remarkable was the fountain gate. This was the one Christ entered in triumph when He rode on the donkey from Bethany. The sheep gate was also located on this side. It took its name from the multitude of sheep that were driven through it for the sacrifice at the temple. The garden was located close to this gate. When they arrested Christ, they led Him through this gate as a sheep to the slaughter. Between the garden and the city ran the brook Kedron. When Christ walked to the garden,

He passed over this brook (John 18:1). The psalmist alludes to this when he writes, "He shall drink of the brook in the way: therefore shall he lift up the head" (Ps. 110:7).

Christ did not enter this garden to hide from His enemies. Judas knew Christ would be there (John 18:2). Christ does not go there to avoid the enemy but to meet the enemy. He goes there to offer Himself as prey to the wolves. He also goes there for an hour or two of privacy before they arrive, that He might freely pour out His soul to God.

It was at the close of evening, for it was after they had finished celebrating the Passover and the supper. Christ likely crossed the brook into the garden between the hours of nine and ten in the evening. So, He had two and three hours to pour out His soul to God. It was about midnight when Judas and the soldiers arrived. When they come, they find Christ upon His knees, wrestling mightily with God in prayer. These were His final moments in the world, and they were employed in prayer.

### The Content of Christ's Prayer

"Father, if thou be willing, remove this cup from me; nevertheless not my will, but thine, be done" (Luke 22:42). Bitter trials and afflictions are frequently expressed in Scripture under the metaphor of a cup (Ps. 11:6; Ezek. 23:32–33). When an affliction is compounded of many bitter ingredients, stinging and aggravating considerations and circumstances, then it is said to be mixed. There is a cup, full of red wine, in the hand of the Lord. It is fully mixed, and He pours it out upon the wicked. "Awake, awake, stand up, O Jerusalem, which hast drunk at the hand of the LORD the cup of his fury; thou hast drunken the dregs of the cup of trembling, and wrung them out" (Isa. 51:17). Christ's cup was a cup of wrath. It was a deep cup that contained more wrath than any creature has ever tasted. It was also a mixed cup—all the bitter aggravating circumstances that could ever be imagined was the portion of His cup.

When Christ prays, "remove this cup from me," He is speaking of the horrid and dreadful wrath of God that He foresaw. The passing away of the cup denotes freedom from those miseries. And so Christ is saying, "Father, if it is Your will, excuse Me from this dreadful wrath. My soul is amazed at it. Is there no way to shun it? If it is possible, spare Me!" This is the meaning of His request. But here is the difficulty: how could Christ, who had agreed with the Father in the covenant of redemption to drink this cup (John 18:37), now ask to be excused from it? Did He now repent of His engagement? Does He regret having undertaken such a work? Is that the meaning of His request? No. Christ never repented of His engagement to the Father. He was never willing to let the burden lie on us rather than on Him. There was no such thought in His holy and faithful heart. The resolution of this doubt depends upon two important distinctions.

For starters, we must distinguish between two kinds of prayer: absolute and conditional. "Remove this cup from me: nevertheless not my will, but thine, be done." This is a conditional prayer. But some will object that Christ knew the mind of God in this case, and He knew the transaction that existed between Him and His Father; therefore, His prayer (though not absolute) is still strange. This brings us to the second distinction. We must distinguish between the natures according to which Christ acted. He acted sometimes as God and sometimes as man. Here He acted according to His human nature, simply expressing His reluctance to suffer. He showed Himself to be a true man by shunning that which is destructive to His nature.

As Christ had two distinct natures, so He had two distinct wills. In the life of Christ, there was a mixture of power and weakness, of divine glory and human frailty. Thus, as a man He feared and shunned death, but as the God-man He willingly submitted to it. There was nothing sinful in His request, because it was a pure and sinless affection of nature. There was actually much good in it because it was a part of His satisfaction for our sin, in that He suffered inwardly such fears, tremblings, and consternations. It was a clear evidence that He was in all things made like unto His brethren, except sin. Lastly, it serves to express the grievousness of Christ's sufferings. The prospect and appearance of them even from a distance was dreadful to Him.

### The Manner of Christ's Prayer

Let us now consider the manner how Christ prayed. First, it was a *solitary* prayer. He does not pray in the audience of His disciples but goes a distance from them. He had private business to transact with God. He left some of them at the entrance to the garden. Peter, James, and John went farther with Him than the rest, but He bids them to remain behind while He prays. He did not desire them to pray with Him or for Him. He must tread the winepress alone. He does not want them with Him, possibly because it would discourage them to see and hear how He cried, groaned, and trembled, as one in an agony, to His Father.

Second, it was a *humble* prayer. This is evident by His posture. At times He is kneeling, and at times He is prostrate on His face. He creeps in the very dust. His heart is as low as His body. He is meek and lowly indeed.

Third, it was a *repeated* prayer. Christ prays, and then returns to His disciples. Having been denied deliverance, He goes to His friends and complains bitterly to them: "My soul is exceeding sorrowful, even unto death" (Matt. 26:38). He would ease Himself a little by opening His condition to them. But they increase His burden, for He finds them asleep. "What, could ye not watch with me one hour?" (Matt. 26:40). Christ finds no comfort in them, and back again He goes to that sad place which He had stained with a bloody sweat. He again prays to the same purpose. He turns again to God, as if He were resolved to take no denial. But, considering it must be so, He sweetly falls in with His Father's will.

Fourth, it was an *agonizing* prayer. "And being in an agony he prayed more earnestly: and his sweat was as it were great drops of blood falling down to the ground." It is disputed whether this sweat was natural or supernatural. I say it must be a supernatural thing for Him to sweat such streams through His garments. What an extraordinary load pressed His soul at that time—even the wrath of a great and terrible God! "Who can stand before his indignation? and who can abide in the fierceness of his anger? his fury is poured out like fire, and the rocks are thrown down by him" (Nah. 1:6).

The effects of this wrath, as it fell upon Christ's soul in the garden, are emphatically expressed by the gospel writers. Matthew tells us that His soul was "exceeding sorrowful, even unto death" (Matt. 26:38). Mark says that He began "to be sore amazed, and to be very heavy" (Mark 14:33). Luke uses another expression: "being in an agony" (Luke 22:44). John records Christ's words as follows: "Now is my soul troubled" (John 12:27). This was the load that so oppressed His soul with fear and grief that the pores of His body were opened to give vent by letting out streams of blood. All the while, no human hand was upon Him. This was but a prelude to the conflict that was at hand. He stood (as it were) arraigned at God's bar and had to deal immediately with Him.

### Application

*Lesson 1*

Prayer is a great relief under the greatest troubles. The best posture for wrestling with affliction is upon our knees. Christ hastened to the garden to pray, when Judas and the soldiers were hastening to arrest Him. When danger is near, it is good to draw near to God. "Be not far from me; for trouble is near; for there is none to help" (Ps. 22:11). Griefs are eased by groans. It is some relief to share our complaints with a faithful friend, but it is a far greater relief to pour out our complaints to a faithful God who can actually help us. We can go to God when we are full of sorrow and our heart is ready to burst, and we can say, "Father, this is my case. I will not complain to others. It serves no purpose to do so. I will tell You, my Father, how the case stands with me. Lord, I am oppressed. Help me!" If we have had any experience in this, we know there is nothing like it. Blessed be God for appointing such an ordinance as prayer!

*Lesson 2*

We should not be discouraged when no answer comes to our prayers. Christ was not heard the first time or the second time. Even the third time, He was not answered as He desired—that the cup might pass from Him. Yet He does not entertain any hard thoughts against God, but resolves His will to His Father's. If God denies the things we ask, He deals with us as He did with Christ. "O my God, I cry in the day time, but thou hearest not; and in the night season, and am not silent. But thou art holy" (Ps. 22:2–3). Christ was not heard in the thing He desired, and yet heard in that He feared (Heb. 5:7). The cup did not pass as He desired, but God upheld Him and enabled Him to drink it. He was heard in that God supported Him, but He was not heard as to exemption from suffering. His will was expressed conditionally; therefore, though He did not receive what He desired, His will was not crossed by God's denial.

When we come before the throne of grace, and cry to God again and again, and no answer comes, we complain, "When I cry and shout, he shutteth out my prayer" (Lam. 3:8). We judge by sense, according to what we see and feel. We struggle to live by faith in God when He seems to hide Himself and refuses our requests. It calls for Abraham's faith, to believe "against hope," giving glory to God (Rom. 4:18). If we cry, and no answer comes, our carnal reason draws a hasty conclusion: "God is angry with my prayers." We need to remember that God hears our prayers though His answer is delayed. As David acknowledged, "I said in my haste, I am cut off from before thine eyes; nevertheless thou heardest the voice of my supplications when I cried unto thee" (Ps. 31:22). A prayer sent up in faith, according to the will of God, is never lost, though it might be delayed.

## Lesson 3

It is a dreadful thing to fall into the hands of the living God, for He is a consuming fire. Christ staggered when the cup came to Him. Did He sweat clots of blood on account of it, and do we make light of it? If it made Him groan, it will make us howl. Sinner, do you make light of the threatening of God's wrath against sin? Look at the face of the Son of God, full of drops of blood under the sense and apprehension of it! Hear how He cries, "Father, if it be possible, let this cup pass!" Hear what He tells the disciples: "My soul is exceeding sorrowful, even unto death." Fools make a mockery of sin and the wrath that hangs over it.

## Lesson 4

We have great cause to love our dear Lord Jesus with an abounding love. We must open the eyes of our faith and fix them upon Christ. We must see Him as He lay in the garden, drenched in His own blood. O what He suffered on our account! It was our pride, sensuality, unbelief, hardness of heart that laid on more weight when He sweat blood.

# 6

# The Nature of Christ's Death

*Him, being delivered by the determinate counsel and fore-knowledge of God, ye have taken, and by wicked hands have crucified and slain.*  —ACTS 2:23

Having considered the preparative acts for Christ's death, we now come to consider His death itself. It was the principal part of His humiliation, and it is the chief pillar of our consolation. According to this verse, Christ's death was violent: He was "crucified and slain." The principal cause (permitting, ordering, and disposing it) was "the determinate counsel and foreknowledge of God." There was not an action or circumstance that did not come under His most wise and holy counsel and determination. The instrumental cause (effecting it) was their "wicked hands." The "counsel and foreknowledge of God" in no way forced or necessitated them to do it, nor did it excuse their act from the least aggravation of its sinfulness. It does not excuse their action from one circumstance of sin, because God's end and manner of acting was most holy and pure, while their end and manner of acting was most malicious and wicked.

*Doctrine: Christ was not only put to death, but to the worst kind of death, even death on a cross.*

The apostle testifies to this: He "became obedient unto death, even the death of the cross" (Phil. 2:8; see also Acts 5:30). Let the following details be weighed. First, it was a *violent* death. It was violent in itself, though voluntary on Christ's part. "He was cut off out of the land of the living" (Isa. 53:8). And yet He laid down His life, meaning no one took it from Him (John 10:17). Christ's death was violent because it was unnatural. He was in the prime of His life, and there was no sin in Him to open the door to natural death. In addition, His death was violent because it was sacrificial. That which dies on its own cannot be offered to God. Only that which is slain, when in its full strength and health, is an acceptable sacrifice.

Second, it was a *painful* death. The apostle speaks of Christ's "pains" (Acts 2:24). His senses were more acute and delicate than ordinary, and they continued to be so in all His suffering. They were never dulled or blunted. Christ's death contained the greatest pains imaginable because they were intended to equal all the misery that our sin deserved. Imagine His plight as all the pains of the damned meet at once in His person!

Third, it was a *shameful* death. He was stripped naked, and so exposed as a spectacle of shame. Moreover, He was condemned to that death which was appointed for the vilest of people. This was a death appointed for slaves. And yet He not only endured the cross but despised the shame (Heb. 12:2). Obedience to His Father's will, and zeal for our salvation, made Him despise the shame and baseness that were in it.

Fourth, it was a *cursed* death. Christ was "made a curse for us: for it is written, Cursed is every one that hangeth on a tree" (Gal. 3:13). The symbol of suspending Him between heaven and earth carries much shame in it, for it implies that He was so vile that He no longer deserved to touch the surface of the earth. And the command to bury Him the same day implied that He was such an abominable sight that He was to be removed as soon as possible from before the eyes of others.

Fifth, it was a *lingering* death. To hang for a long time in the midst of tortures, and to feel every ounce of pain, is indeed a misery. Surely, in this respect, it was worse for Christ than anyone who was ever nailed to a cross. While He hanged there, He remained full of life and acute sense. His life did not depart gradually but was wholly in Him to the last. Other people die gradually, and their sense of pain is much blunted toward the end. They expire by degrees. But Christ stood under the pains of death in His full strength. This was evident by the mighty cry He made when He breathed His last. It caused the centurion to conclude, "Truly this man was the Son of God" (Mark 15:39).

Sixth, it was a *helpless* death. Sometimes they gave malefactors, in the midst of their torments, some vinegar and myrrh to dull their senses. If they hanged there for a long time, they would break their bones to dispatch them out of their pain. Christ had none of this.

Christ came to take away the curse from us by His death, and so He must be made a curse. All the curses of the moral law (which were due to us) must lie on Him.

## Application

*Lesson 1*

There is forgiveness for the greatest of sinners. "In whom we have redemption through his blood, even the forgiveness of sins" (Col. 1:14). "The blood of Jesus Christ his Son cleanseth us from all sin" (1 John 1:7). There is sufficient efficacy in the blood of the cross to expiate and wash away the greatest sins. It is called "precious" blood (1 Peter 1:19) because of the union it has with that person who is over all, God blessed forever. On that account, it is described as the blood of God (Acts 20:28). The blood of all the creatures in the world, even a sea of human blood, bears no more proportion to Christ's precious blood than a dish of common water to a river of liquid gold. On account of its inestimable value, it is satisfying and reconciling blood to God (Col. 1:20). The same blood, which is redemption to those who dwell on earth, is confirmation to those who dwell in heaven. Before the efficacy of this blood, guilt vanishes as the shadow before the glorious sun. Every drop of it has a voice, and it speaks (to the person who sits trembling under its guilt) better things than the blood of Abel (Heb. 12:24). It sprinkles us clean from an accusing conscience (Heb. 10:22). Having enough in it to satisfy God, it must have enough in it to satisfy the conscience.

As there is sufficient efficacy in this blood to expiate the greatest guilt, so it is manifest that its virtue is intended and designed by God for the use of believing sinners. "And by him all that believe are justified from all things, from which ye could not be justified by the law of Moses" (Acts 13:39). The remission of the sins of believers was the great thing designed in the pouring out of Christ's precious blood. This appears from all the Old Testament sacrifices. The shedding of that typical blood spoke of God's design to pardon. And the putting of their hands upon the head of the sacrifice spoke of the way and method of believing, by which that blood was then applied.

Moreover, this blood of the cross is the blood of a surety who came under the same obligations with us. Christ shed His blood in our place and so of course frees and discharges the principal offender (Heb. 7:22). Can God exact satisfaction from the blood of His Son, the surety of believers, and yet still demand it from believers? No. "Who shall lay any thing to the charge of God's elect? It is God that justifieth. Who is he that condemneth? It is Christ that died" (Rom. 8:33–34). God calls upon sinners to repent and believe in this blood, encouraging them to do so with many precious promises of remission. This speaks of the possibility of a pardon for the greatest sinner. It speaks of the certainty of a full, free, and final pardon for all believing sinners. O what a joyful sound is this! The Word assures us that the darkest and deepest sins have been washed away in this blood. The apostle Paul was "a blasphemer, and a persecutor, and injurious," yet he "obtained mercy" (1 Tim. 1:13).

*Lesson 2*

While there is much pain in death, there is no curse in the believer's death. It strikes, but it has lost its sting by which it destroys. A snake that has no venom can hiss and threaten, but we can take it in our hand without any danger. Death lost its sting in Christ's side when He became a curse for us. As there is no curse in death, so there are many blessings in it.

Death is ours as a special favor and privilege (1 Cor. 3:22). Christ has not only conquered it but He has made it beneficial and serviceable to the saints. When Christ was nailed to the cross, He said (as it were) to death: "O death, I will be your plague! O grave, I will be your destruction!" And so He was, for He swallowed up death in victory and spoiled it of its power. Though it may still frighten some weak believers, it cannot hurt them.

*Lesson 3*

We can cheerfully bear any cross for Christ. He had His cross, and we have ours. But our crosses are feathers compared to His. His cross was heavy indeed, yet He supported it patiently and meekly. Three facts will marvelously strengthen us to bear our cross. First, we bear the cross for a little while. It is true that Christ and His cross are inseparable in this life. But Christ and His cross part ways at heaven's door, for there is no room for crosses in heaven. Not a tear, sigh, fear, loss, or trouble can find lodging there. Life is but short, and therefore crosses cannot be long. Our sufferings are only for a little while (Rom. 8:18; 1 Peter 5:10).

Second, Christ bears the heaviest end of the cross. He divides our sufferings and takes the largest share to Himself. They are called "the afflictions of Christ" and "the reproach of Christ" (Col. 1:24; Heb. 11:26). The cross falls first upon Him, and then merely rebounds from Him to us (Rom. 15:3). Christ does not only bear the better part of the cross, but the whole of it. Yea, He bears all and more than all, for He bears us and our burden, or else we would quickly sink and faint under it.

Third, the cross produces innumerable mercies. Our sufferings are washed in Christ's blood, in that His merit bought a blessing to our crosses. Therefore, we shall die and yet live. I have but small experience of suffering for Christ, but I do find a little paradise of glorious comforts and delights in suffering for Him and His truth. Grace tried is better than grace. It is glory in its infancy.

*Lesson 4*

Our mercies were brought forth with great difficulty. That which is sweet to us was costly to Christ in acquiring it. The price of blood hangs over every mercy (Col. 1:14). Life comes through death. The choicest mercies come through the greatest miseries. Prime favors come to us swimming in blood (Rev. 1:5). O we should use this to raise the value of our mercies! We must not abuse any of the mercies that Christ brought forth with so many bitter pangs. And let all this endear Christ more than ever to us and make us in a deep sense of His love to say, "Thanks be to God for Jesus Christ!"

# 7

# A Lonely Death

*Awake, O sword, against my shepherd, and against the man that is my fellow, saith the* LORD *of hosts: smite the shepherd, and the sheep shall be scattered: and I will turn mine hand upon the little ones.*
—ZECHARIAH 13:7

In the former sermon, we explained how Christ's innocence was vindicated by the honorable title providentially affixed to the cross. Now we will consider how He endured the cross. As evident from our verse, He did so alone (see also Matt. 26:31). There are four things to consider.

First, the commission given to the sword: "Awake, O sword...smite." God can open all the armories in the world with the word of His mouth. He can command whatever weapons and instruments of death He pleases. Here, He calls for the sword, which opens the door to death and destruction. Its strokes and thrusts are mortal. And He bids it "awake." The term signifies both to rouse up from sleep and to rouse up with triumph and rejoicing (Job 31:29). God commands it to "awake" and "smite." It is as if He said, "Come forth from your scabbard, O sword of justice! You have been hidden for a long time, asleep in your scabbard. Now, awake and glitter! You will drink royal blood, such as you have never shed before."

Second, the person against whom the sword is commissioned: "my shepherd, and…the man that is my fellow." This shepherd can be none other than Christ, who is often described in Scripture as the Shepherd (John 10:11; 1 Peter 5:4). God also refers to Him as His fellow (or His neighbor). And so Christ is God's fellow with respect to His unity and equality with the Father, both in essence and will. We have the sense of it in Philippians 2:6: He was "in the form of God, [and] thought it not robbery to be equal with God." The sword receives its commission against Christ—God's fellow, the delight of His soul.

Third, the dismal result of this deadly stroke upon the shepherd: "the sheep shall be scattered." By "sheep" we understand the little flock of the disciples, who followed this Shepherd until He was smitten—that is, apprehended by His enemies. At that hour, they scattered. They all forsook Him and fled. And so Christ was left alone, amid His enemies.

Fourth, the gracious mitigation of this sad dispersion: "I will turn mine hand upon the little ones." The "little ones" are His sheep. The expression is intentionally varied to show their weakness and feebleness, which appeared in their scattering from Christ. God turns His hand "upon" them, meaning He graciously gathers them after their dispersion, so that none of them are lost. After Christ was risen, He went before them into Galilee (Matt. 26:32), where He gathered them again by a gracious hand, so that not one of them was lost but the son of perdition.

*Doctrine: Christ's dearest friends forsook Him in the time of His greatest distress and danger.*

Who were these sheep who were dispersed and scattered from their Shepherd when He was smitten? It is evident that they were those precious elect souls whom He had gathered to Himself and whom He dearly loved. They had left everything to follow Him. Until that moment, they had faithfully continued with Him in His temptations (Luke 22:28). They were all resolved to do so (Matt. 26:35). But they all forsook Him and fled from Him. This was not a total and final apostasy—that is, the fall of the hypocrite. They were stars fixed in their orb, though clouded for a time. Their scattering was but a mist that covers the earth in the morning until the sun rises and then disappears and gives way to a fair day. Though it was not a total and final apostasy, it was a very sad and sinful relapse from Christ.

**The Cause of Their Fall**

The reasons for their relapse are manifold. First, God permitted it by suspending the needed influences of grace from them. They would not have scattered if there had been influences of power, zeal, and love from heaven upon them. Christ must not receive the least relief or comfort from any creature. And so God withholds His encouraging and strengthening influences from them for a time so that Christ might be left alone to grapple with God's wrath. "Be strong in the Lord, and in the power of his might" (Eph. 6:10). If that strength is withheld, our resolutions and purposes melt away before temptation as snow before the sun.

Second, the efficacy of the temptation was stronger than normal. As they were weaker than usual, so the temptation was greater than anything they had ever encountered. It is called "the power of darkness" (Luke 22:53). O it was a black day! The disciples had never met with such a furious storm. The devil desired to sift and winnow them so that their faith might utterly fail. But Christ secured them by means of His prayer for them. O it was an extraordinary trial that was upon them!

Third, the remaining corruptions in their hearts, yet unmortified, led to their scattering. Their knowledge was little and their faith was weak. On account of their weakness in grace, they were called "little ones." As their graces were weak, so their corruptions were strong. Their carnal fears grew powerfully within them. But let us not censure them in our thoughts nor despise them for their weakness. They did not plan to do this, and their souls detested it. Here we see just how far those who fear God may be carried if their corruptions are irritated by strong temptations and God withholds His influences.

### The Result of Their Fall

Their scattering ended far better than it began. Though these sheep were scattered for a time, Christ kept His promise by turning His hand toward them to gather them. The morning was cloudy, but the evening was clear. Peter repents of his denial of Christ, and he never denied Him again. The others also returned to Christ, and they never forsook Him again. They openly confessed Him before councils and rejoiced that they were counted worthy to suffer for His sake (Acts 5:41).

They were as fearful as hares but became as bold as lions. They sealed their confession of Christ with their blood. Though they forsook Him, they still loved Him. Though they fled from Him, a gracious principle still remained in them. Though they forsook Christ, He never forsook them. He still loved them. "Go your way, tell his disciples and Peter that he goeth before you into Galilee: there shall ye see him" (Mark 16:7). That is, "Do not let them think that I so remember their unkindness as to no longer own them. I still love them!"

**Application**

*Lesson 1*

The disciples forsook Christ despite their strong persuasions and resolutions that they never would. Here we see that self-confidence is a sin found in the best people. The disciples never thought their hearts would have proved so vile and deceitful. "Though all men shall be offended because of thee," says Peter, "yet will I never be offended." He resolved honestly, but he did not know what a feather he would be in the wind of temptation. Left to themselves, the angels quickly fell from their own habitations (Jude 6). Every excellency, without the support of divine preservation, is but a weight that tends to a fall. What becomes of the stream without the fountain? The constant supplies of the Holy Spirit are the food and fuel of all our graces.

We should never be self-confident, given these examples of human frailty. What match are we for principalities, powers, and spiritual wickedness? "Be not highminded, but fear" (Rom. 11:20). We ought to consider the examples of Noah, Lot, David, and Hezekiah—men of renown who fell by temptation.

Did such men fall? Then "let him that thinketh he standeth take heed lest he fall" (1 Cor. 10:12).

*Lesson 2*

Christ stood His ground when everyone forsook Him. A resolved adherence to God and duty, without company or encouragement, is truly excellent. Elijah complains, "The children of Israel have forsaken thy covenant, thrown down thine altars, and slain thy prophets with the sword; and I, even I only, am left; and they seek my life, to take it away" (1 Kings 19:10). And yet all this did not discourage him from following the Lord, for he was still very jealous for the Lord of hosts. Paul complains, "At my first answer no man stood with me, but all men forsook me.... Notwithstanding the Lord stood with me" (2 Tim. 4:16–17). As the Lord stood by Paul, so Paul stood by his God without any support from others. He who professes Christ for company will also leave Him for company. If we can, it is sweet to travel to heaven in the company of saints who are on the way with us. But if we meet no company, we must not be discouraged.

*Lesson 3*

The disciples forsook Christ, but they were restored. Believers are not beyond backsliding, but they are secure from final apostasy. Saints may fall, but they will rise again (Mic. 7:8). The highest flood of natural zeal might dry up, but saving grace is a well of water, "springing up into everlasting life" (John 4:14). God's unchangeable election and Christ's prevalent intercession give believers abundant security against the danger of a total and final apostasy. "My Father, which gave them me, is greater than all; and no man is able to pluck them out of my Father's hand" (John 10:29; see also 2 Tim. 2:19). Every person committed to Christ by the Father will be brought by Him to the Father.

God has so framed and ordered the new covenant that none of those souls who are within its blessed bond can possibly be lost. It is settled upon immutable things (Heb. 6:18–19). Among the many glorious promises is this: "I will not turn away from them, to do them good; but I will put my fear in their hearts, that they shall not depart from me" (Jer. 32:40). As the fear of God in our hearts pleads in us against sin, so our powerful Intercessor in heaven pleads for us with the Father. For this reason, we cannot finally miscarry (Rom. 8:34–35).

*Lesson 4*

We are strong or weak according to the decrees of assisting grace. Sometimes we are bold and courageous, despising dangers and enduring discouragements, in the strength of zeal and love for God. At other times we are faint, feeble, and discouraged at every petty thing. This difference arises from the different administrations of the Holy Spirit, who sometimes gives more and sometimes gives less of His gracious influence. We cannot take the just measure of a Christian by one act, neither can we judge of ourselves by what we sometimes feel. When our spirits are low and our hearts are discouraged, we should say to ourselves, "Hope in God: for I shall yet praise him" (Ps. 43:5).

*Lesson 5*

The sword was drawn against the Shepherd, and He was left alone to receive its mortal strokes. We should adore the justice and mercy of God, which are so illustriously displayed in this. Here is the triumph of divine justice—to single out the Shepherd, the man who is God's fellow, and plunge its sword into His breast for satisfaction. No wonder it is brandished with such a triumph! It has more glory in His shed blood than if the blood of all the men and women in the world had been spilt. The mercy and goodness of God are no less manifested in the giving of a commission to the sword against the Shepherd. He could have said, "Awake, O sword, against those who are My enemies! Shed their blood and scatter them, for they have sinned against Me!" Blessed be God that the dreadful sword was not brandished against us and that He did not bathe it in our blood! Blessed be God that His fellow was smitten, so that His enemies might be spared! O what manner of love is this! Blessed be God for Jesus Christ! He received the fatal stroke for us, and God has now sheathed the sword in its scabbard so that it will never be drawn against those who believe in Christ.

*Lesson 6*

The dreadful sword of divine justice smote the Shepherd, and at the same time the flock was scattered from Him. We learn that the holiest people have no reason to despond if God should strip them of all their comforts. God sometimes removes outward comfort and leaves inward comfort; sometimes He removes inward comfort and leaves outward comfort. But the time may come when God strips us of both. This was the case with Job, who was blessed with outward and inward comforts. Yet the time came when God took everything from him.

If the Lord chooses to do the same to us, the following considerations will be helpful. First, it is nothing new. God has so dealt with others, yea with Christ who was His fellow. Second, Christ passed through such conditions on purpose so that He might remove the curse and leave the blessing for us. Third, despite the loss of inward and outward comforts, God remains with us (John 16:32). He supports us when all sensible comforts shrink away from the soul and body. Fourth, Christ's comfortless condition preceded the day of His greatest glory and comfort. The most glorious light usually follows the thickest darkness. The louder our groans are now, the louder our triumphs will be then. The horror of our present will but add to the luster of our future state.

# 8

# A Lowly Death

*He was oppressed, and he was afflicted, yet he opened not his mouth: he is brought as a lamb to the slaughter, and as a sheep before her shearers is dumb, so he openeth not his mouth.*
—ISAIAH 53:7

We are considering the manner of Christ's death. His loneliness in His suffering was the subject of the last sermon. Christ's meekness in His suffering is the subject of this one. Isaiah describes Christ's suffering and its blessed fruit. Such is the clearness of his prophecy that he is deservedly called the "evangelical prophet." There are two parts in our verse.

First, Christ's grievous suffering: "He was oppressed, and he was afflicted…he is brought as a lamb to the slaughter." Christ stood before God as a surety before the creditor. God exacted the utmost satisfaction from Him by causing Him to suffer according to the utmost rigor and severity of the law. It did not suffice that He was shorn as a sheep (i.e., stripped of His riches, comforts, and ornaments), but He also had to give His blood and life. He is brought to the slaughter.

Second, Christ's meek and patient spirit: "as a sheep before her shearers is dumb, so he openeth not his mouth." The lamb goes as quietly to the slaughterhouse as to the fold. By this lively and lovely similitude, Christ's patience is here expressed to us. Yet Christ's silence is not to be understood simply, as though He spoke nothing at all when He suffered. He uttered many weighty and excellent words upon the cross, but He never opened His mouth complainingly, vehemently, or vindictively.

*Doctrine: Christ supported the burden of His sufferings with admirable patience and meekness of spirit.*

It is true that meekness invites injury but triumphs in the end. This was verified in Christ's suffering. His meekness triumphed over His enemies' affronts and injuries much more than they triumphed over Him. Patience never had a more glorious triumph than it had upon the cross. Christ's meekness of spirit amid injuries and provocations is excellently set forth in 1 Peter 2:22–23: "Who did no sin, neither was guile found in his mouth: who, when he was reviled, reviled not again; when he suffered, he threatened not; but committed himself to him that judgeth righteously." There are three things to consider.

### The Object of Christ's Patience

The burden of Christ's sufferings and provocations was very great. All sorts of trouble gathered upon Him. There were troubles in His soul. He was laden with spiritual horrors. He began to be "sore amazed, and to be very heavy" (Mark 14:33). The wrath of an infinite God beat Him down to the dust. There were also troubles in His body. It was full of pain and torture in every part. Every member of His body was the seat and subject of torment. His name and honor suffered the vilest indignities, blasphemies, and reproaches that Satan and wicked people could belch out. He was called a blasphemer, glutton, drunkard, and friend of publicans and harlots. Contempt was poured upon all His offices. They mocked His kingly office when they crowned Him with thorns, arrayed Him with purple, bowed the knee to Him, and cried, "Hail, King of the Jews." They mocked His prophetical office when they blindfolded Him and bid Him prophesy who smote Him. They mocked His priestly office when they reviled Him on the cross, saying, "He saved others; himself he cannot save" (Matt. 27:42).

Now all this, and much more than this, met at once upon His innocent and dignified person. He was greater than all, and He could have crushed all His enemies as a moth. For Him to bear all this, without the least discomposure of spirit, is the highest triumph of patience that the world has ever seen. It is a great wonder.

### The Nature of Christ's Patience

Patience is a power to suffer hard and heavy things, according to the will of God. There are three parts to this definition. First, patience is a power. It is a passive fortitude whereby we are "strengthened with all might, according to his glorious power, unto all patience and longsuffering with joyfulness" (Col. 1:11). The loss of our patience under adversity points to a decay of strength in the soul. "If thou faint in the day of adversity, thy strength is small" (Prov. 24:10).

Second, patience is a power to suffer hard and heavy things. God has several sorts of burdens to impose upon His people. Some are heavy and some light. Some are to be carried for a few hours and some for many days. Some are internal and some external. Sometimes God imposes both at the same time. That was the case with Christ. His soul was burdened by the full sense and apprehension of the wrath of God, while His body was filled with tortures in every member. Here was the highest exercise of patience.

Third, patience is a power to suffer hard and heavy things, according to the will of God. In this respect, the Christian grace of patience differs from the moral virtue of patience. The apostle speaks of those who "suffer according to the will of God" (1 Peter 4:19). They are to exercise patience graciously, as God would have them. When this is the case, our patience is like Christ's. It extended itself to every trouble and affliction that came upon Him. "Innumerable evils have compassed me about" (Ps. 40:12). Yet He had patience to receive them all. His patience was as large as His trouble. It was full of submission, peace, obedience, and contentment in His Father's will. As was His external behavior, so too was His internal frame of soul. No discontents, murmurings, or despondencies had a place in His heart.

## The Cause of Christ's Patience

Let us inquire into the grounds of Christ's perfect patience. The first is His perfect holiness. His nature was free from those corruptions that afflict our nature. Moses excelled all others in meekness, yet even he spoke "unadvisedly with his lips" (Ps. 106:33). Job's patience is trumpeted all over the world, yet even he cursed the day he was born. Envy, revenge, discontent, and despondency are weeds that naturally grow in the corrupt soil of our nature (James 4:5). Because the principle of these evils is in our nature, they will show themselves in the time of trial. But it was otherwise with Christ. His nature is like a pure crystal glass, full of pure fountain water, which though shaken and agitated does not contain any dregs. "The prince of this world cometh, and hath nothing in me" (John 14:30). There was no principle of corruption in Him, to give a handle to temptation. Our high priest was holy, undefiled, and separate from sinners (Heb. 7:26).

Second, Christ's patience proceeded from the infinite wisdom with which He was filled. Wise people are patient people. Meekness is a fruit that arises from the root of wisdom (James 3:13). In contrast, anger is lodged in folly (Eccl. 7:9). As wise Solomon has observed, "A man of understanding is of an excellent spirit" (Prov. 17:27). Now, wisdom filled the soul of Christ. In Him are hid "all the treasures of wisdom" (Col. 2:3). Hence, He was unmoved by His enemies' abuse.

Third, Christ's patience flowed from His foreknowledge. He had a perfect view of all those things from eternity that befell Him in time. They did not come upon Him by surprise. And, therefore, He did not wonder at them when they came, as if some strange thing were happening to Him. He foresaw all these things long before they took place (Mark 8:31). He had agreed with His Father to endure all this suffering for our sakes (Isa. 50:6). Knowing what He must suffer, and having agreed to do so, He bore that suffering with great patience. "Jesus therefore, knowing all things that should come upon him, went forth, and said unto them, Whom seek ye?" (John 18:4).

Fourth, Christ's patience sprang from His faith. He looked through all those black and dismal clouds to "the joy that was set before him" (Heb. 12:2). He knew that though Pilate would condemn Him, God would justify Him (Isa. 50:4–8). He balanced His future glory against His present suffering. He set His faith upon God for divine support and assistance under suffering as well as for glory (Ps. 16:7–11). This filled Him with peace.

Fifth, Christ's patience arose from the Holy Spirit, who filled Him with a heavenly tranquility and calmness of spirit. It is a certain truth that the more heavenly any person's soul is, the more composed and peaceful it is. Certainly, the heart that is sweetened frequently with delightful communion with God is not very apt to be embittered with wrath or soured with revenge. The heavenly soul marvelously affects a quiet heart. There has never been a more heavenly soul on earth than Christ's. He had sweet communion with God. He was in heaven upon earth (John 3:13) in respect of the heavenly communion He had with God. His heart was in heaven when He so patiently endured the pain and shame of the cross (Heb. 12:2). His eye was on "the joy" when He went as a lamb to the slaughter.

Sixth, Christ's patience sprang from His complete and absolute obedience to His Father's will and pleasure. He could most quietly submit to all the will of God and never regret any part of the work assigned to Him. His death was an act of obedience (Ps. 40:6–8; John 18:11; Phil. 2:7–8). He was privy to His Father's purpose; therefore, He was able to see the Jews and Gentiles as mere instruments in the fulfillment of God's pleasure, serving His great design.

Seeing as there is nothing more defective in believers and prejudicial to religion than a lack of patience, I resolve to persuade you to pursue it. We are called to this (1 Peter 2:21–22).

## Application

*Lesson 1*

We look upward to see the sovereign Lord who sends troubles upon us. They do not emerge from the dust, but descend from heaven (Jer. 18:11). They are the Lord's instruments to bring His wandering people to Himself. In the frame of our afflictions, we can observe divine wisdom in their choice, measure, and season. We see God's sovereignty in choosing the instruments of our affliction, in making them as afflictive as He pleases, and in making them obedient to His call. If we could look up to this sovereign hand in times of trouble, our hearts would be quiet. "It is the LORD: let him do what seemeth him good" (1 Sam. 3:18). When we look no higher than people, our hearts swell with impatience. But if we see people as a rod in our Father's hand, we will be quiet (Ps. 46:10). It is our failure to look up to God in our troubles that causes us to fret, murmur, and despond.

*Lesson 2*

We look downward to see what is below us. We tend to think no one has suffered like us and that there is no trouble like ours. We must look at others. Do we not see that others are in a far more miserable state than us? What is our affliction? Have we lost a relation? Others have lost families. Have we lost an estate? Others have lost everything. Are we persecuted for Christ's sake? Others have suffered far worse (Heb. 11:36–38). Are our afflictions more spiritual and inward? What do we think of Job, David, Asaph, and others? The Almighty was a terror to them; the arrows of God pierced them; they roared by reason of the trouble of their hearts. Are our afflictions in soul and body? So it was with Job and many other worthies who have gone before us. Surely we may see many on earth who are in a far lower and sadder condition than us. Surely there are many in hell who would gladly trade their condition for ours. When we see all those who are below us, we will recognize that we have plenty of reasons to be quiet.

*Lesson 3*

We look inward to see if we can find something to quiet us. (1) What do we see of corruption? Does our proud heart need humbling? Does our carnal heart need mortifying? Does our wandering heart need recovering? "If need be, ye are in heaviness through manifold temptations" (1 Peter 1:6). Do we not see the need of this present trouble? God knows we are ruined without it. Our corruptions require troubles to kill them. (2) What do we see of grace? The Lord has planted the principles of faith, humility, patience, and joy in our souls. Does the Lord intend for them to remain in their drowsy habits? Or does He intend for us to exercise them? How can we do this without tribulations? "Tribulation worketh patience; and patience, experience; and experience, hope" (Rom. 5:3–4). When we look inward, we will be quiet.

*Lesson 4*

We look outward to see who stands by us, observing our conduct under trouble. There are many evil eyes upon us (Ps. 5:8). For the wicked, there is no higher pleasure than to see that our conduct under trouble is just like theirs, for thereby they are confirmed in their prejudices against religion and in their good opinion of themselves. Do we merely talk of heaven's glory and future expectations? Do we dishonor Christ before His enemies when we make them think that all our religion lies in talk?

*Lesson 5*

We look backward to see if there is something in our past experience that might quiet our impatient hearts. Is this the first difficulty we have ever experienced? We have been in trouble before, and the Lord has helped us. O what cause do we have to be impatient? Did He help us then, and will He not help us now? "This I recall to my mind, therefore have I hope" (Lam. 3:21). Have we kept no records of past experiences? How ungrateful then have we been to our God and how injurious to ourselves! Past experiences were given to us for this reason. When we consider what God has been to us, how faithfully He has stood by us, how repeatedly He has raised us up, surely we will find strength in the midst of our present troubles.

*Lesson 6*

We look forward to see the end of our troubles. (1) We look to the end of their duration. They are not eternal. "But the God of all grace, who hath called us unto his eternal glory by Christ Jesus, after that ye have suffered a while, make you perfect" (1 Peter 5:10). These light afflictions are "but for a moment" (2 Cor. 4:17). What are they in comparison to the vast eternity that is before us? What are a few days and nights of sorrows once they are gone? Are they not swallowed up as a spoonful of water in the vast ocean? (2) We look to the end of their operation. What do all these afflictions effect? Do they not result in an exceeding weight of glory? Do they not make us partakers of His holiness? Why would we be impatient on their account? God is using them to perfect our happiness.

# 9

# A Prayer for Forgiveness

*Then said Jesus, Father, forgive them; for they know not what they do.*
                                                                —LUKE 23:34

While Christ was on the cross, words dropped from His lips and blood dropped from His wounds. In this way, He exercised His offices of prophet and priest, instructing us by His words and redeeming us by His blood. Christ's seven statements from the cross are His last words, with which He breathed out His soul. They are remarkable. Three are directed to His Father and four to those around Him.

The first statement is in our verse: "Father, forgive them; for they know not what they do." It contains three noteworthy particulars. First, Christ's request: "forgive them." Forgiveness is one of the greatest mercies we can obtain from God. "Blessed is he whose transgression is forgiven, whose sin is covered" (Ps. 32:1). Second, the people for whom Christ prays—namely, those who crucified Him. He desires the best of mercies for the worst sinners. Third, the argument Christ uses to procure God's mercy: "they know not what they do."

Their sin is not so much out of malice to the Son of God as ignorance of the Son of God (Acts 3:17; 1 Cor. 2:8).

In what sense were they ignorant of Christ? They were a knowledgeable people in many things. They knew many truths, but they did not know Christ. "Blindness in part is happened to Israel" (Rom. 11:25). They had natural light, but they had no knowledge that He was the Son of God and the Savior of the world. How is this possible? They were eyewitnesses of His miraculous works. They knew something of His birth, life, and death. They were familiar with the prophecies concerning Him. How could they not see that He was the fulfillment of the Scriptures? They had the Scriptures, but they misunderstood them. They expected a glorious Messiah who would come with majesty as the king of Israel. But when they saw Christ in the form of a servant, coming in poverty, they utterly rejected Him. Ignorance enslaves and subjects the soul to the lusts of Satan. He is "the rulers of the darkness of this world" (Eph. 6:12).

It is dreadful to oppose knowingly Christ and His truth. Paul was once filled with rage and madness against Christ and His truth, but he did it ignorantly (1 Tim. 1:13). There is forgiveness with God for those who oppose Christ out of ignorance. If God will forgive all manner of sin and blasphemy, then He will forgive this sin (Matt. 12:31). Even those who crucified Christ may receive remission by the blood they shed (Acts 2:23, 38).

Forgiveness is God's gracious discharge of a believing penitent sinner from the guilt of all his sin for Christ's sake. First, it is God's discharge. There is indeed fraternal forgiveness, whereby we forgive one another (Luke 6:37). There is also ministerial forgiveness, whereby the minister of Christ applies the promises of pardon to penitent offenders (John 20:23). But neither of these can properly and absolutely forgive sin. God alone can forgive sin (Mark 2:7). The principal wrong is done to Him (Ps. 51:4). For this reason, sin is called a debt to God (Matt. 6:12), meaning it obliges us to satisfy the penalty we owe to Him on account of it. Who can pay this debt but God?

Second, it is God's gracious discharge. "I, even I, am he that blotteth out thy transgressions for mine own sake" (Isa. 43:25). God does not expect any satisfaction from us, because He has provided a surety (Christ) for us and He is satisfied in Him: "In whom we have redemption through his blood, the forgiveness of sins, according to the riches of his grace" (Eph. 1:7).

Third, it is God's gracious discharge from the guilt of all sin. Guilt is an obligation to punishment. Pardon is the dissolving of that obligation. Guilt is a chain with which sinners are bound by the law. Pardon breaks the chain and makes the prisoner a free man. The pardoned soul is a discharged soul (Rom. 8:33).

Fourth, it is God's gracious discharge of a believing penitent sinner. Infidelity and impenitency are not only sins in themselves but such sins as bind fast all other sins upon the soul. "By him all that believe are justified from all things" (Acts 13:39). "Repent ye therefore, and be converted, that your sins may be blotted out" (Acts 3:19). This is the method by which God dispenses pardon to sinners.

Fifth, it is God's gracious discharge of a believing penitent sinner for Christ's sake. He is the meritorious cause of our remission. For Christ's sake, God has forgiven us (Eph. 4:32). It is His blood alone that meritoriously procures our discharge.

Why would anyone, who is humbled for their enmity to Christ while in the days of ignorance, question the possibility of forgiveness? There is enough in His blood to pardon our sins and the sins of the whole world (1 John 2:2). There is not only sufficiency but limitless merit in that precious blood. Surely our enmity to Christ, especially before we knew Him, is not an unpardonable sin.

God's Word never excludes this sin from pardon. On the contrary, such is the extensiveness of God's promise to believing penitents that this case is manifestly included (Isa. 60:7). God has forgiven such sinners in the past, and what He has done, He can do again. He has already forgiven some, so that others might be encouraged to hope for the same mercy. The apostle Paul is a famous example of this (1 Tim. 1:13–16). It is a great encouragement to a sick person to hear of others who have recovered from the same disease. Moreover, it is encouraging to consider that when God has cut off others in the way of their sin, He has spared us. This reveals His merciful purpose for us (2 Peter 3:15). He has spared us and given us a heart humbled for our sin. Does not this speak mercy? Surely it looks like a gracious design of God's love for us.

*Doctrine: To forgive enemies, and beg forgiveness for them, is the true character of a Christian.*

This is what Christ did: "Father, forgive them." Stephen imitated Christ in this (Acts 7:59–60). And this is what Christ requires of us (Matt. 5:44–45).

## The Nature of This Duty

I will begin by showing you what Christian forgiveness is not. First, it is not a Stoic insensibility to wrongs and injuries. God has not made us to be stupid blocks who have no sense or feeling of what is done to us. He allows us a tender sense of natural evils, though He will not allow us to avenge ourselves by moral evils. The more tender our resentment of wrongs and injuries is, the more excellent our forgiveness is. A forgiving spirit does not exclude a sense of injuries, but the sense of injuries graces the forgiveness of them.

Second, it is not a polite concealment of our anger because we think we have no choice in the matter. We might fear the reproach if we act otherwise, or we might lack the opportunity to act otherwise. But neither of these is Christian meekness, but the sign of a vile nature.

Third, it is not a moral virtue. It is possible to attain certain virtues without a change in nature (e.g., temperance, patience, and justice). These are of great use to maintain peace and order in the world. Without them, civil societies would soon break apart. Though they are ornaments of nature, they do not reveal a change in nature. True graces do not come by natural acquisition but supernatural infusion.

Fourth, it is not a prejudicial surrendering of our rights and properties to the lusts of everyone who has a mind to invade them. We may lawfully defend our lives and properties. We are bound to do so. If we cannot defend them legally, we must not avenge them unchristianly.

Christian forgiveness is a gentleness of spirit that freely passes by injuries done to us in obedience to God's command. (1) It is a gentleness of spirit. God's grace calms tumultuous passions. "The fruit of the Spirit is love, joy, peace, longsuffering, gentleness" (Gal. 5:22). (2) It is a gentleness of spirit that inclines us to pass by injuries. We do not retain them bitterly in our mind or avenge them when we have the opportunity. As a carnal heart thinks revenge is its glory, the gracious heart is content that forgiveness is its glory. (3) It is a gentleness of spirit that inclines us to pass by injuries in obedience to God's command. Our nature inclines us in another direction (James 4:5). It longs to avenge, but the fear of God represses such motions. God has forgiven us as well as commanded us: "Be ye kind one to another, tenderhearted, forgiving one another, even as God for Christ's sake hath forgiven you" (Eph. 4:32).

**The Excellence of This Duty**

When we can shape our hearts into that heavenly frame to which we are so averse, it points to the excellence of our religion. It is mere morality to hide lusts and passions. But the glory of Christianity is that it mortifies the lusts of nature. When we are meek, humble, and patient, we win glory to our religion. Christianity teaches us to receive evil and return good (1 Cor. 4:12–13). This is the meekness that is fashioned in us by the wisdom that is from above (James 3:17). This stamps the very image of God upon us and makes us like our heavenly Father, who does good to His enemies (Matt. 5:44–45). In a word, this Christian temper of spirit gives us the true possession and enjoyment of ourselves so that our hearts will be as the placid sea, smooth and pleasant, while others are as the raging sea, foaming and casting up dirt and mire.

## Application

*Lesson 1*

There is forgiveness with God for those who have been ene-mies to Christ. Certainly, therefore, there is pardon for the friends of God who involuntarily fall into sin and are broken for it. If God has pardon for His enemies, surely He has par-don for His children. If He has forgiveness for those who shed Christ's blood with wicked hands, surely He has much more mercy for those who love Christ and are afflicted for their sin against Him. We must not doubt it. If God receives enemies into His bosom, then He will embrace His offending children. We are so pensive after we lapse into sin. We wonder if God will pardon us. Will His face look favorably on us as in former times? O if we knew the largeness, tenderness, and freeness of His grace, which has granted pardon to thousands and thou-sands of the worst of sinners, we would never doubt!

*Lesson 2*

Since God pardons His enemies, it is inexcusable to persist and ultimately perish in enmity to Christ. Mercy is offered to them if they will receive it (Isa. 55:7). The gospel proclaims that if any of Christ's enemies repent, and are willing to be reconciled, they will find mercy. The blood of those who per-ish in their enmity to Christ lies at their own door (Ps. 7:2; 68:21). This realization will cut their hearts for eternity: "I could have received pardon, but I refused it! God offered me gracious terms, but I rejected them!"

*Lesson 3*

The Christian religion is the greatest friend to the peace of states and kingdoms. Nothing is more opposite to the true Christian spirit than strife, revenge, tumults, and uproars. It teaches people to do good and receive evil and to receive evil and return good (James 3:17–18). The rule by which believers walk is this: "If it be possible, as much as lieth in you, live peaceably with all men. Dearly beloved, avenge not yourselves, but rather give place unto wrath: for it is written, Vengeance is mine; I will repay, saith the Lord" (Rom. 12:18–19). It is not religion, but lust, that makes the world so unquiet (James 4:1–2). It is not godliness, but wickedness, that makes people bite and devour one another. One of the first effects of the gospel is to civilize those places where it comes and thereby establish peace and order among people.

*Lesson 4*

It is a dangerous thing to abuse and wrong forgiving Christians. Their patience to forgive often invites injury and encourages vile people to trample upon them. But there is nothing in the world that should more frighten people from such practices than this: they may abuse and wrong them, but the Lord will avenge them. "Be patient therefore, brethren, unto the coming of the Lord" (James 5:7). When the Jews put Christ to death, He "committed himself to him that judgeth righteously" (1 Peter 2:23). Did not God severely avenge Christ's blood on them and their children? Yes. Do not they and their children groan under the miserable effects of it to this day? Yes. If God undertakes the cause of His abused people, He will be sure to avenge them in far greater measure than they could ever avenge themselves.

*Lesson 5*

We should imitate Christ and labor for meek and forgiving spirits. Christ's glory is far more than our life and all that we enjoy in this world. We must not expose it to the scorn and derision of His enemies. May they never say, "How is Christ a lamb, when His followers are lions?" We should also seek the peace of our own souls. What is life worth without the comfort of life? What comfort can we have in all that we possess in the world as long as we do not have the possession of our own souls? If our hearts are full of tumult and revenge, the Spirit of Christ will become a stranger to us. He delights in clean and quiet hearts.

# 10

# A Promise of Salvation

*And Jesus said unto him, Verily I say unto thee, Today
shalt thou be with me in paradise.*          —LUKE 23:43

In this statement, Christ expresses the riches of free grace
to the penitent thief—a man who had spent his life in wickedness. His practice had been vile and profane, but now his
heart was broken for it. He is converted—the first fruit of the
blood of the cross. In the preceding verse, this thief manifests
his faith: "Lord, remember me when thou comest into thy
kingdom." In our verse, Christ manifests His pardon and gracious acceptance of him: "Verily I say unto thee, Today shalt
thou be with me in paradise." Let us take note of four things.

First, the *content* of Christ's promise: "Today shalt thou
be with me in paradise." By "paradise" He means heaven—a
place of delight. This is the abode of gracious souls when separated from their bodies at death. Some of the church fathers
vainly imagined that heaven and paradise are different places.
But Paul uses the expressions "third heaven" and "paradise"
to describe the same place (2 Cor. 12:2–4). It is the place of
blessedness designed for God's people (Rev. 2:7). The most

intimate communion with Christ is in heaven, and this is the substance of Christ's promise to the thief.

Second, the *recipient* of Christ's promise: the thief, who had lived lewdly and profanely and was under just condemnation for his crimes. But God gave him a penitent and believing heart, almost at his last gasp, and he was converted in an extraordinary way. Being thus converted, he professed Christ amid the shame of His death, vindicated His innocence, and begged for mercy: "Lord, remember me when thou comest into thy kingdom."

Third, the *fulfillment* of Christ's promise: "Today shalt thou be with me in paradise." Christ informed the thief that he would enjoy blessedness immediately at the time of his dissolution. I object to those who deny an immediate state of glory for believers after death. They read Christ's statement thus: "Verily I say unto thee today, Thou shalt be with me in paradise." They place the comma so as to make the word *today* refer to the time Christ made the promise rather than the time He fulfilled the promise. People can make the Scriptures speak anything! There is no doubt that Christ, in this expression, fixes the time of the thief's happiness: "Today shalt thou be with me."

Fourth, the *confirmation* of Christ's promise: "Verily I say unto thee." No higher security can be given. Christ is able to perform what He promises because heaven is His. He is faithful to His promises and has never forfeited any of them.

*Doctrine: At their death, all believers are immediately received into a state of glory and eternal happiness.*

## The Certainty of the Future State

This truth is a principal foundation to our hope and happiness. Seeing as our hope is only as strong as its foundation, I will establish this truth by five arguments. First, the existence of God proves it. Since there is a God who rules the world, He must rule it by rewards and punishments, equally and righteously distributed to the good and the bad. He must make a difference between the obedient and disobedient, the righteous and the wicked. To make creatures capable of a moral government, and not to rule them, is to make them in vain. As He has made rational creatures, capable of moral government by rewards and punishments, so He rules them in that way which is suitable to their natures, promising it will be well with the righteous and ill with the wicked (Isa. 3:10–11). These promises and threats are not merely intended to frighten us. They are not empty but contain real danger or benefit. Every word of God must be fulfilled.

Second, the content of Scripture confirms it. The Bible contains the system of laws for the government of humanity, which the wise and holy Ruler of the world has ordained for that purpose. In them we find promises made to the righteous of a full reward in the next life for all their obedience, patience, and suffering. We also find threats made against the wicked of eternal wrath and anguish in hell as the just recompence for their sin (Rom. 2:5–10; 2 Thess. 1:4–7). We could add multitudes of Scriptures to these plain testimonies. Heaven and earth will pass away, but these words will never pass away.

Third, the testimony of conscience reveals it. Where is the person whose conscience never felt any impressions of hope or fear from the prospect of a future world? If it is said that these are but the effects of sermons or education, I ask how the consciences of heathens, who have neither Scriptures nor preachers, are impressed with these things (Rom. 2:15)? If there were no such things as heaven and hell, the conscience would never accuse or excuse for good or evil done in this world.

Fourth, the death of Christ requires it. Why did He come into the world if there is no future state? Why did He assume our nature and suffer such terrible things? Our comforts are raised by our expectation of the happiness to be enjoyed in heaven. But if there is no heaven to which we are appointed, and no hell from which we are redeemed, we comfort ourselves with a fable. Surely, the purpose of Christ's death was to deliver us from the wrath to come (1 Thess. 1:10) and to bring us to God (1 Peter 3:18). In sum, His purpose was to be the author of eternal salvation to those who obey Him (Heb. 5:9).

Fifth, the immortality of the soul settles it. The human soul vastly differs from that of an animal, which is but a material form and therefore perishes with its matter. It is not so with us. Our rational soul can live and act in a separated state from our body (Eccl. 3:21). If people dispute whether they are rational, their very disputing proves them to be so.

## The Immediacy of the Future State

"Today shalt thou be with me." Some have taught that there is indeed a future state of happiness or misery but that we do not pass into it immediately when we die; rather, our soul sleeps until the resurrection and then awakens and enters into its body. Are souls so wounded by their separation from the body that they cannot subsist apart from them? Is such an idea of soul-sleep found anywhere in the Scriptures? No. The Scriptures record no such interval but plainly deny it. "We are confident, I say, and willing rather to be absent from the body, and to be present with the Lord" (2 Cor. 5:8). "For I am in a strait betwixt two, having a desire to depart, and to be with Christ; which is far better" (Phil. 1:23). If the soul sleeps until the resurrection, then how is it far better to "depart" than to live? Surely, if the soul sleeps, Paul's state in the body would be far better than his state after death.

To defend their position, they appeal to Christ's words in John 14:3: "If I go...I will come again, and receive you unto myself." They argue that Christ receives His people to Himself at His second coming at the end of the world. Even though Christ will then collect all believers into one body and present them to His Father, this in no way hinders Him from receiving every believing soul to Himself at death. If this is not the case, then how can the Scriptures speak of Him coming to judgment accompanied with a host of His saints (Jude 14). The Scriptures do not place an interval between the death of a saint and his glorification. Rather, it speaks of the saints who are dead as already being with the Lord and of the wicked who are dead as already in hell (Luke 16:22; Acts 1:25; 1 Peter 3:19–20).

But let us weigh four additional arguments in order to resolve this point. First, why should our happiness be deferred, since we are capable of enjoying it as soon as we are separated from the body? "We are confident, I say, and willing rather to be absent from the body, and to be present with the Lord" (2 Cor. 5:8). When we part from the body, we go home to the Lord. The entanglements of the soul are so great and so many in its embodied state that it cannot freely take in the comforts of God by communion with Him. Surely, the freeing of the soul from that burden cannot be an impediment to its greater happiness.

Second, why should the soul's happiness be deferred, unless God had some additional preparative work for it? But, surely, there is no such work after its separation from the body by death. When the body is dissolved, all means, duties, and ordinances cease. Our glorification is not deferred in order to make us fully prepared for glory. If we are not fit when we die, we will never be fit. All is done upon us that ever was intended to be done. We are called "the spirits of just men made perfect" (Heb. 12:23).

Third, why should our salvation slumber, when the damnation of the wicked does not slumber? God does not defer their misery, and surely He will not defer our glory. If He is quick with His enemies, He will not be slow with His friends. He is as inclined to acts of favor to His children as He is to acts of justice to His enemies (Acts 1:25; 1 Peter 3:19–20; Jude 7).

Fourth, how are such delays consistent with Christ's ardent desire to have His people with Him where He is? We see the reflected flames of desire of mutual enjoyment between the Bridegroom and His spouse in Revelation 22:17–20. Delays make their hearts sick. The expectation in which the saints die is to be satisfied then, and surely God will not deceive them. I do not deny that their glory will be more complete when the body is resurrected, reunited with the soul, and made to share in its happiness. But that does not hinder the soul from enjoying glory while the body sleeps in the dust.

**Application**

*Lesson 1*

There is an eternal state into which souls pass after this life. This means time is precious, and we must make the most of it. God has set a great weight on a small wire. How we use these few hours will determine how we are in eternity. Every day, every hour, every moment of our present life has an influence upon our eternity. Do we believe this? Yet we squander away precious time so carelessly. How can we do it? Surely our wastefulness in using our time reveals that we have but little sense of the great eternity that lies before us.

*Lesson 2*

The difficulties of religion, which serve to promote our eternal happiness, are most rational. The disproportion between now and eternity, things seen and things unseen, the vanishing present and the eternal future, is so vast. We can never be wise until we let go of the best enjoyments on earth when they stand in the way of eternal happiness. We can never escape the just censure of folly if we gratify our appetites at the expense of eternal glory in heaven. Moses chose "to suffer affliction with the people of God, than to enjoy the pleasures of sin for a season" (Heb. 11:25). No one considers him to be a fool who spends a penny to gain thousands of dollars. But, surely, the disproportion between now and eternity is much greater.

*Lesson 3*

There is an eternal state into which souls pass immediately after death. This ought to effect a great change in us. O what a serious thing it is to die! It is our passage out of the swift river of time into the boundless and bottomless ocean of eternity. Our souls are (as it were) now asleep in their bodies; but at death they awake and find themselves in the world of realities. Let this teach us how to carry ourselves toward dying people when we visit them and to make provision every day for our dying hour. We must be serious, simple, and faithful with those who are stepping into eternity, and we must be the same with our soul every day. We need to remember that eternity is an amazing thing.

*Lesson 4*
Believers are immediately with God after their death. The suddenness and greatness of the change will be amazing to our thoughts. We are here in the body, conversing with people and living among material objects, and then suddenly with the Lord in heaven, standing among an innumerable company of angels and the spirits of the just made perfect. What a change is this! In a mere wink of the eye, we will be transferred in the arms of angels into the invisible world. We will live without eating or drinking. We will be lifted up from a bed of sickness to a throne of glory, from a sinful and troublesome world to a place free from all troubles and struggles. We cannot think what this will be like. Who can tell what sights, thoughts, and apprehensions believing souls will have when they are removed from the eyes of their surviving friends?

*Lesson 5*
Believers are immediately with God after their dissolution, but unbelievers will find themselves in another state once death has closed their eyes. What will be their case? They

will be plucked out of house and body, from among friends and comforts, and thrust into endless miseries, into the dark vault of hell. They will never again see the light of this world. They will never again see a comfortable sight, hear a joyful sound, or know the meaning of rest, peace, or delight. They will exchange the smiles and honors of people for the frowns and fury of God. They will be clothed with flames and drink the pure unmixed wrath of God. We may say of them, "Hell from beneath is moved for thee to meet thee at thy coming: it stirreth up the dead for thee" (Isa. 14:9). There will be no more sports, plays, cups of wine, or beds of pleasure. The more they enjoyed these here, the more intolerable will this change be to them. If saints are immediately with God, others must be immediately with Satan.

*Lesson 6*

Those who will be with God so soon after their death have little cause to fear. Some tremble at the thoughts of death, but those who have an interest in Christ do not need to fear. We lose nothing by death. The words *death*, *grave*, and *eternity* should have another kind of sound in our ears, and they should make contrary impressions upon our hearts. If our earthly tabernacles cast us out, we will not be found naked. We have "a building of God, an house not made with hands, eternal in the heavens" (2 Cor. 5:1). It is but a step out of this world into heaven. O what sweet and lovely thoughts we should have of that great and final change!

# 11

# A Cry of Forsakenness

*And about the ninth hour Jesus cried with a loud voice, saying, Eli, Eli, lama sabachthani? that is to say, My God, my God, why hast thou forsaken me?*
—MATTHEW 27:46

This verse contains the fourth saying of Christ from the cross. These words are able to break the hardest heart in the world. It is the voice of the Son of God in agony. His suffering was great before but never in the extremity as it is now, when this heaven-rending and heartmelting cry broke from Him: "Eli, Eli, lama sabachthani?" There are three noteworthy details in this cry.

First, the *time* of Christ's cry: "about the ninth hour." This means it was about three in the afternoon. The evangelist marks this on purpose to show us how long Christ was in distress upon the cross: three hours.

Second, the *matter* of Christ's cry: "My God, my God, why hast thou forsaken me?" He does not cry because of the cruel tortures to His body or the reproaches to His name. He seems to ignore all these and only complains of what was more burdensome than ten thousand crosses—His Father's desertion. It is an inward trouble that burdens Him as God hides His face from Him. He had never known such an affliction until now.

Third, the *manner* of Christ's cry: "Jesus cried with a loud voice." He did not cry like a dying man in whom nature was spent, but as one full of life, sense, and vigor. He stirred up the whole power of nature when He made this grievous cry. We see the vehemence of His cry, in that He says, "My God, my God, why hast thou forsaken me?" It is as if He were surprised by the strangeness of this affliction. Stirring Himself with unusual zeal, He turns to the Father and cries, "Why so, My Father? What do You mean by this? Why do You hide Your face from Me in the depth of My torments and troubles?"

*Doctrine: Designing to heighten Christ's suffering to the uttermost, God forsook Him in the time of His greatest distress, to the unspeakable anguish of His soul.*

### The Nature of the Desertion

Divine desertion is God's withdrawing His love, grace, and favor from an individual. When these are gone, God is said to be gone. He withdraws in two ways. The first is *absolutely* and *permanently*. There are some (such as the fallen angels) who were once in God's love and favor, but they have utterly and finally lost it. God is so withdrawn from them that He will never again take them into His favor. The second way is *respectively* and *temporarily*. God sometimes forsakes His dearest children by removing all the sweet manifestations of His love and favor for a time. He acts like a stranger to them, though His love remains the same. This second kind of desertion serves various ends. Probational desertion is for the purpose of proving and trying grace. Cautional desertion is designed to prevent sin. Disciplinary desertion is God's rod to chastise His people for sin. Penal desertion is inflicted as the just reward of sin. Christ experienced this last kind of desertion in that He bore the curse to make satisfaction for our sins.

For the better understanding of Christ's cry of desertion, we must consider the following points. First, it does not mean that He dissolved the personal union of the two natures. When He was forsaken by God, He was still true and real God-man in one person.

Second, it does not mean that the Father pulled away the prop of divine support from Him by which He had (until then) endured the tortures and sufferings that oppressed Him. Though the Father deserted Him, He still supported Him. God was with Him by way of support when He was withdrawn as to the manifestations of His love and favor. In respect of God's supporting presence, it is said, "Behold my servant, whom I uphold" (Isa. 42:1; see also John 16:32).

Third, it does not mean that God left Him as to inherent grace and sanctification, recalling the Spirit of holiness who had anointed Him. When Christ was forsaken, He remained as holy as ever. He had indeed less comfort but not less holiness. Without this holiness, His sacrifice could never have yielded such a fragrant aroma to God (Eph. 5:1–2).

Fourth, it does not mean that God's love was so withdrawn from Christ that the Father no longer had any love for Him or delight in Him. That would be impossible. He can no more cease to love Christ than to love Himself. His love was not turned into wrath, though now His wrath alone was manifested to Him as our surety. He hid His love from Him as His beloved Son.

Fifth, it does not mean that Christ was finally forsaken by His Father. The dark cloud dwelt upon His soul for only a few hours. It soon passed away, and the bright and glorious face of God shone forth again as bright as ever (Ps. 22:1, 24).

Sixth, it does not mean that there was a mutual desertion—a desertion on both parts. The Father forsook Christ, but Christ did not forsake His Father. When God withdrew, Christ followed Him, crying, "My God, my God."

Seventh, it was a sad desertion. Christ's other sufferings were small compared to this. They bore upon His body, but this upon His soul. They came from the hands of vile people, but this from the hand of a dear Father. He suffered both in body and soul, but the suffering of His soul was the very soul of His suffering. Under all His other sufferings He never opened His mouth, but this touched Him so that He cried out, "My God, my God, why hast thou forsaken me?"

Eighth, it was a penal desertion. It was inflicted on Him to make satisfaction for our sins. Christ's cry was like the perpetual shriek of those who are cast away forever. This was that hell (and the torments of it) which Christ, our surety, suffered for us. As there lies a twofold misery upon the damned in hell, pain of sense and pain of loss, so Christ experienced an impression of wrath and a withdrawal of all sensible love and favor. Hence, He declares, "Now is my soul troubled" (John 12:27)—troubled as those who are in hell. God did not leave His soul in hell, because He had enough to pay the debt we owed. Yet His suffering in His soul upon the cross was equivalent to all that we should have suffered in hell for eternity.

Ninth, it was a real desertion. Christ does not impersonate a deserted soul, speaking as if God had withdrawn the comfortable sense and influence of His love. It really happened. The Godhead restrained and withheld, for this time, all its joy, comfort, and sense of love from the manhood, yielding it nothing but support. Christ's bitter and painful cry gives evidence enough of its reality. He did not fake it; rather, He felt the burden of it.

Tenth, it was a desertion that occurred at the time of Christ's greatest need for comfort. His Father forsook Him at that time when all earthly comforts had forsaken Him and all outward evils had broken upon Him. When pain, shame, and misery weighed Him down, even then, God withdrew to fill and complete His suffering.

Eleventh, it was a desertion that left Christ to the support of His faith. He had nothing else to rest upon but His Father's covenant and promise. And indeed, Christ's faith manifests itself in these words of complaint in our verse. His comfortable sense of God's love is obstructed, yet His soul clings to Him: "My God, my God." Faith speaks first: "My God." Then, sense speaks: "Why hast thou forsaken me?" His faith prevented the complaint of sense. Although sense comes with a word of complaint, there are two words of faith ("My God, my God") to one word of sense. As His faith spoke first, so it spoke twice, when sense and feeling spoke but once. And as faith spoke first, so it spoke more confidently than sense did. He lays a confident claim to God as His God and only queries about His forsaking of Him. "Why hast thou forsaken me?" This is spoken more doubtfully, while the former is spoken more confidently.

In short, Christ's faith took hold of God under a most suitable title: "Eli, Eli"—literally, "My strong One, My strong One!" He leans on the One to whom belongs infinite strength, the One who had supported His manhood and, according to His promise, had upheld Him. This desertion left Christ with only these supports of faith. By these things He stood, when all other visible and sensible comforts shrunk away from His soul and body.

## The Purpose of the Desertion

God's design in this desertion was twofold: satisfaction and sanctification. It made satisfaction for our sins, which deserved that we should be totally and everlastingly forsaken by God. This is the just reward of every sin. The damned feel it and will do so for eternity. God is not gone from them essentially, for the God of power and justice is with them forever. The avenging God is always with them. But the merciful God is gone forever. And thus He would have withdrawn Himself from every sinner if Christ had not borne that punishment in His own soul: "My God, my God, why hast thou forsaken me?" Apart from Christ, we would have howled this hideous complaint in hell forever: "O righteous God! O dreadful God! O terrible God! You have forsaken me!"

The desertion of Christ also sanctified all the desertions experienced by the saints. Having been forsaken before us and for us, Christ turned God's forsaking of us into a mercy—hence all the precious fruits and effects of our desertions. We are stirred to pray (Ps. 88:1, 9), remember the past (Ps. 77:5), and value the divine presence with the soul (Song 3:1–5). These (and many more) are the precious effects of sanctified desertion. We owe them all to Christ, who is their author. He passed through this sad and dark state for our sakes, that we might find these blessings in it.

Therefore, the Godhead's suspending of all the effects of joy and comfort from the humanity of Christ upon the cross is a special part of Christ's satisfaction for us, and consequently, that which makes all our temporary desertions to be mercies rather than curses.

### The Effect of the Desertion

Let us turn our attention to the effect of this desertion upon Christ. It did not drive Him to despair, yet it amazed Him and almost swallowed up His soul in the depths of trouble and alarm. His astonishing cry arises from a soul oppressed to death. That we might appreciate that there has never been a sorrow like Christ's in this deserted state, let us consider the following details.

First, it was a *new* burden. Christ had never experienced anything like this before. From all eternity until now, there had been constant and wonderful outlets of love, joy, and delight from the bosom of the Father into His bosom. He had never seen a frown or veil upon that blessed face. This made it a heavy burden indeed. His words declare His astonishment: "My God, my God, why hast thou forsaken me?" That is to say, "You have never done this before. Why are You doing it now?"

Second, it was a *great* burden. It was so great that He scarce knew how to support it. If it had not been so great, He would never have drooped under it and complained of it. It was so sharp and heavy that it caused Him, who was as meek as a lamb under all other suffering, to roar like a lion.

"My God, my God, why hast thou forsaken me? why art thou so far from helping me, and from the words of my roaring?" (Ps. 22:1). The term comes from a root that signifies to howl or roar as a lion. It signifies the noise made by a wild beast. It is as much as if Christ had said, "O, My God, no words can express My anguish. I will not speak, but roar out My complaint." It is no small matter that makes Him roar. His spirit was so great that He would not have roared under a slight burden. When His body was in tortures, and all about Him was full of horror and darkness, and He stood in great need of divine support and comfort, He fell into this desertion.

Third, it was a *prolonged* burden. It lasted from the time His soul became sorrowful in the garden until His death. We could not bear to hold a finger in the fire for two minutes. But what is the finger of a man to the soul of Christ? What is physical fire to the wrath of God?

Fourth, it was a *heavy* burden. In all probability it hastened Christ's death. It was unusual for crucified persons to expire so quickly, and those who were crucified with Him were still alive when He died. But no one has ever felt what Christ felt inwardly. He bore it until the ninth hour, and then He made a fearful cry before dying.

### Application

*Lesson 1*

God forsook Christ upon the cross as a punishment for our sins. This means that, as often as we sin, we deserve to be forsaken by God. This is the just recompense for sin. Indeed, here lies the principal evil in sin: it makes a separation between God and the soul. This separation is due to the moral evil that is in it and the penal evil inflicted by the righteous God for it. By sin we depart from God and, as a due punishment, God departs from us. This will be the dismal sentence in the last day: "Depart from me, ye cursed" (Matt. 25:41). A chasm will be fixed between God and sinners. The eternal shriek of the damned is this: "Alas, God has forsaken us for eternity! Ten thousand worlds can never make up for the loss of God!" Beware, those of you who say to God, "Depart from us! We do not desire the knowledge of Your ways." One day, He will say to you, "Depart from Me! You shall never see My face."

*Lesson 2*

Christ never complained until God hid His face from Him. This teaches us that the hiding of God's face is the greatest misery that can befall a gracious soul in this world. When they scourged and buffeted Christ, and when they nailed Him to the cross, He did not open His mouth. But when His Father hid His face from Him, He cried out. His voice was the cry of roaring. This was more to Him than a thousand crucifixions. Surely it is the same for all gracious souls. When God hides His face, it is the saddest stroke and heaviest burden. We moan, "Why am I redeemed, called, and reconciled, if I cannot see the face of my God?"

Have tears ever trickled down our cheeks when we have looked toward heaven and were unable to see the face of our God? We mourn bitterly when the Lord, who is the life of our life, departs for a season from us. If God departs, our sweetest enjoyment on earth, the very crown of all our comforts, is gone. What can recompense a saint for the loss of his God? If we had never seen the Lord, or tasted the incomparable sweetness of His presence, then it would be another matter. But the darkness that follows the sweetest light of His countenance is a double darkness.

The horror of this darkness is increased because Satan, who is like a wild beast in the desert, creeps out of his den and roars upon us with hideous temptations. Surely, this is a sad state and it deserves tender compassion. If you have ever been in trouble like this, you will never slight others in the same case. One purpose of God's exercising us with troubles of this nature is to teach us to be compassionate toward others in the same case. "Have pity upon me, have pity upon me, O ye my friends; for the hand of God hath touched me" (Job 19:21). We must be merciful and compassionate toward them, for we have been in the same case.

*Lesson 3*
The desertion of Christ affords great comfort to God's people. It prevents our final desertion. Because He was forsaken for us, we will never be forsaken. God's forsaking Him, though only for a few hours, is equivalent to His forsaking us for eternity. It is as much for the dear Son of God to be forsaken by God for a time as it is for poor sinners to be cast off for eternity. That being the case, it ought to give us the greatest security in the world. God will never finally withdraw from us. If He had intended to do so, Christ would never have made such a cry from the cross: "My God, my God, why hast thou forsaken me?"

In addition to affording comfort, the desertion of Christ provides a comfortable pattern to poor deserted souls. How? First, God deserted Christ, yet He continued to support Him.

His omnipotent arms were under Him, though His face was hid from Him. Christ did not have God's smile, but He had His support. It is the same with us. Our God may turn away His face, but He will not take away His arm.

Second, God deserted Christ, but Christ did not desert God. His Father forsook Him, but He could not forsake His Father, but followed Him with this cry: "My God my God, why hast thou forsaken me?" Is it not the same with us? God goes off from our soul, but we cannot go off from Him. Our heart mourns after the Lord, seeking Him carefully with tears, complaining of His absence as the greatest evil in this world. This is Christlike.

Third, God forsook Christ, but He returned to Him again. It was but for a time. God might, for wise and holy reasons, hide His face from us, but not as He hides it from the damned. In our case, the cloud will pass. The night will have a bright morning. "For I will not contend for ever, neither will I be always wroth: for the spirit should fail before me, and the souls which I have made" (Isa. 57:16). It is as if He should say, "I may contend with him for a time to humble him, but I will not do so forever." O the tender compassion of a displeased Father!

Fourth, God forsook Christ, but Christ justified God. "O my God, I cry in the day time, but thou hearest not; and in the night season, and am not silent. But thou art holy" (Ps. 22:2–3). Is our soul framed like Christ's in this? We can say, even when God writes bitter things against us, that He is good, holy, and faithful. We are deserted but not wronged. There is not one drop of injustice in the sea of our sorrows. Though He condemns us, we will justify Him. This too is Christlike.

Fifth, God took from Christ all visible and sensible comforts (inward as well as outward), but Christ subsisted by faith in the absence of them all. His desertion put Him upon the acting of His faith. "My God, my God." These are words of faith—the words of One who depends completely upon God. Is it not so with us? Is the sense of God's love gone? Are the sweet sights of God shut up in a dark cloud? What then? Will our hands hang down and our soul give up all hope? Is there no faith to relieve us? Yes, there is. "Who is among you that feareth the LORD, that obeyeth the voice of his servant, that walketh in darkness, and hath no light? let him trust in the name of the LORD, and stay upon his God" (Isa. 50:10).

Sixth, Christ was deserted a little before the glorious morning of light and joy dawned upon Him. It was but a little after this sad cry that He triumphed gloriously. It may be so with us. Heaviness may endure for a night, but joy and gladness will come in the morning. We must be resolved to wait for Him, cleave to Him, and mourn after Him.

*Lesson 4*

God forsook His Son upon the cross. This means the dearest of God's people may for a time be forsaken by their God. We must not think it is strange when we, who are the children of light, meet with darkness. We must not charge God for dealing harshly with us. We see what happened to Christ. We should expect and prepare for days of darkness. We have heard Christ's painful cry. We know how it was with Job, David, Heman, Asaph, and many others. What heartmelting lamentations they made upon this account! Are we better than they are? O prepare for spiritual troubles! If this trial befalls us, we should give attention to these two admonitions.

First, we must exercise the faith of adherence when we have lost the faith of evidence. When God takes away the second, He leaves the first. It is sweet to live in views of our interest. But, if they are gone, we must rely on God for our interest. We rest in God when we have no light (Isa. 50:10). We drop this anchor in the dark and do not reckon that all is gone when evidence is gone. We never reckon ourselves to be undone while we can adhere to our God. Direct acts of faith are noble acts of faith, so too are reflexive ones. (1) As our comfort depends on the evidencing acts of faith, so our salvation depends upon the adhering act of faith. Evidence comforts, but adherence saves. Salvation is more than comfort. (2) Our faith of evidence has more sensible sweetness, but our faith of adherence is more constant and continual. (3) Faith of evidence brings more joy to us, but faith of adherence brings more glory to God, for thereby we trust Him when we cannot see Him. We believe against sense and feeling. Doubtless, that which brings glory to God is better than that which brings comfort to us.

Second, we must take the right method to recover the sweet light which we have sinned away from our souls. We do not go about complaining, nor sit down desponding under our burden. (1) We search diligently after the cause of God's withdrawal. We urge Him by prayer to tell us why He contends with us (Job 10:2). "Lord, what have I done that so offends Your Spirit? I plead with You to show me the cause of Your anger. Have I grieved Your Spirit in this or in that? Was it my neglect of duty or my formality in duty? Was I not thankful for the sense of Your love when it was shed abroad in my heart? O Lord, why is it thus with me?" (2) We humble ourselves before the Lord for every evil He shows us. We tell Him that it pierces our hearts that we have so displeased Him. We invite Him again to our soul and mourn after Him until we have found Him. If we seek Him, we will find Him. (3) We wait in the use of means until Christ returns. O we must not be discouraged! Though God tarries, we wait for Him. Blessed are those who wait for Him!

# 12

# A Cry of Anguish

*After this, Jesus knowing that all things were now accomplished, that the scripture might be fulfilled, saith, I thirst.*
—JOHN 19:28

When Christ labored in the agonies of death, He said, "I thirst." He uttered these words a little before "he bowed his head, and gave up the ghost" (v. 30). There are two kinds of thirst: natural and spiritual. Christ felt both. His soul thirsted, in vehement desires and longings, to accomplish His great work. His body thirsted by reason of its unparalleled agonies. When He said, "I thirst," He intended this natural thirst.

Of all the pains and afflictions of the body, there is scarcely anything more intolerable than extreme thirst. The mightiest have stooped under it. It is used to express an afflicted state: "When the poor and needy seek water, and there is none, and their tongue faileth for thirst, I the LORD will hear them" (Isa. 41:17). Thirst causes a painful compression of the heart, when the body, like a sponge, seeks to draw in moisture, but there is none. And this may be compounded by a lack of water or by laboring under grievous agonies and extreme tortures. Christ's thirst was caused by the extreme sufferings that He had endured in His soul and body.

The end of Christ's complaint was "that the scripture might be fulfilled." Whatever was predicted by the prophets was exactly accomplished by Christ. "They gave me also gall for my meat; and in my thirst they gave me vinegar to drink" (Ps. 69:21).

*Doctrine: Christ's agonies and sufferings upon the cross were such that He cried, "I thirst."*

### Christ's Physical Agony

Christ's corporeal and external sufferings were exceedingly great. First, they were acute. His body was racked in the more sensitive parts where pain and anguish meet. "They pierced my hands and my feet" (Ps. 22:16). By reason of His excellent temper of body, Christ had more tender and delicate senses than other people. His body was so formed that it might be a spacious vessel to take in more suffering than any other body could. His body was miraculously formed on purpose to suffer unparalleled miseries and sorrows. "A body hast thou prepared me" (Heb. 10:5). Neither sin nor sickness dulled it in any way.

Second, Christ's sufferings were universal. They seized every member of His body from head to foot. His head was wounded with thorns, His back with lashes, and His hands and feet with nails. His body was stretched beyond its natural length by hanging upon that cruel engine of torment—the cross. Every particular sense was afflicted. His sight was afflicted with the vile wretches and cruel murderers who stood around Him, His hearing with horrid blasphemies, His taste with vinegar and gall, His smell with that filthy Golgotha where He was crucified, and His feeling with exquisite pains in every part.

Third, Christ's sufferings were continual. He did not experience a moment's relief from His pain. Wave came upon wave, one grief driving another, until all God's waves and billows had gone over Him.

Fourth, Christ's sufferings were unrelieved. If a person has sweet comforts, flowing into his soul from God, his physical pain will be alleviated. This made the martyrs shout in the midst of the flames. Even inferior comforts and delights of the mind will greatly relieve the oppressed body. But Christ had no relief in this way. Not a drop of comfort came from heaven into His soul to relieve Him. On the contrary, His soul was filled with grief, and it had a heavier burden to bear than that of the body. Instead of relieving, it increased unspeakably the burden of His outward man.

### Christ's Spiritual Agony

Christ's inward suffering was great. First, His soul felt the wrath of an angry God, which was terribly pressed upon Him. The wrath of a king is as the roaring of a lion, but what is the wrath of God? "Who can stand before his indignation? and who can abide in the fierceness of his anger? his fury is poured out like fire, and the rocks are thrown down by him" (Nah. 1:6). If the strength that supported Christ had not been greater than that of rocks, this wrath would certainly have overwhelmed Him and ground Him to powder.

Second, Christ's soul felt the pure wrath of God. It was without one drop of comfort from heaven or earth. All the ingredients in His cup were bitter. It was wrath without the least degree of sparing mercy. God "spared not his own Son" (Rom. 8:32). If Christ had been spared, we could not be. If our mercies must be pure mercies, and our glory in heaven pure and unmixed glory, then the wrath that He suffered must be pure and unmixed wrath.

Third, Christ's soul felt the full wrath of God. There is not one drop for the elect to feel. Christ's cup was deep and large. It contained all the fury and wrath of an infinite God. And yet He drank it. To those who make peace with God through Christ, He says, "Fury is not in me" (Isa. 27:4). In all the chastisements God inflicts upon His people, there is no vindictive wrath. Christ bore it all in His own soul and body on the cross.

Fourth, Christ's soul felt the aggravated wrath of God. It went beyond what the damned suffer. You might think this is strange. How can there be any sufferings worse than those the damned suffer? An infinite God holds them up with the arm of His power, while the arm of His justice lies on them eternally. Can any sorrow be greater than this? Yes. Christ's suffering was greater in a number of ways. The damned do not suffer innocently as Christ suffered. They do not have the capacity to take in the full sense of God's wrath as Christ did. They were never so near and dear to God as Christ was.

## Christ's Complaint

It is evident that such extreme physical and spiritual sufferings, meeting together upon Christ, caused Him to cry, "I thirst." Here we see what external pain and outward affliction can do. They consume our spirits. "When thou with rebukes dost correct man for iniquity, thou makest his beauty to consume away like a moth" (Ps. 39:11). As a moth consumes the strongest garment and makes it rotten, so afflictions waste and wear out the strongest bodies. They dry up the most vigorous and flourishing body and make it shrivel like a bottle in the smoke (Ps. 119:83). We also see what troubles of the soul can do to the strongest body. They spend its strength. "A broken spirit drieth the bones" (Prov. 17:22; see also Ps. 32:3–4). Finally, we see that, when physical pains meet with spiritual troubles, the strongest body wastes away.

If the body is sick and full of pain, the soul strengthens it by means of reason and resolution. If the soul is afflicted, the body sympathizes with it and supports it. But if the body is overcome with strong pains and the soul is oppressed with intolerable anguish, they are unable to help one another. Instead, each increases the other's burden. When this happens, nature must fail and the friendly union between soul and body suffers dissolution. This is what happened to Christ when outward and inward sorrows met in their extremity upon Him. Hence, He cried, "I thirst."

## Application

### Lesson 1

Sin is a horrid thing. If all this must be suffered to expiate it, then it must be a great evil. Christ's suffering for sin gives us a true account and full representation of its evil. Let us imagine that the bars of the bottomless pit were broken and the damned spirits ascended with the chains of darkness rattling at their heels. We hear their groans. We see the trembling of those poor creatures upon whom the righteous God has impressed His fury and indignation. We hear how their consciences are lashed by the fearful scourge of guilt and how they shriek at every lash received from the arm of justice. If we could see and hear all this, it would be nothing compared to what we see in this verse. The Son of God, under His suffering, cried out, "I thirst." His suffering was well beyond that of the damned. O we must not trifle with sin, as if it were but a small thing! When we see the face of sin in Christ's agony, we discover that there is no more horrid thing in all the world. Fools mock at sin, but the wise tremble at it.

*Lesson 2*

Inward troubles are intolerable. Christ complained so sadly under them. Surely, then, they are not such light matters as many people tend to make of them. If they so scorched the very heart of Christ, we dare not make light of them. He was fitted to bear and suffer the strongest troubles that ever befell human nature. He bore all other troubles with admirable patience. But when it came to this, when the flames of God's wrath scorched His soul, He cried, "I thirst."

David was courageous and had the heart of a lion. But when God touched him with inward troubles for sin, he roared under the anguish: "I am feeble and sore broken: I have roared by reason of the disquietness of my heart.... My heart panteth, my strength faileth me: as for the light of mine eyes, it also is gone from me" (Ps. 38:8, 10). Many have professed that all the torments in the world are mere trifles compared to the torment of the soul. The racking fits of the gout and the grinding tortures of the stone are nothing in comparison to the wrath of God upon the conscience. What is the worm that never dies but the torment of a guilty conscience? This worm gnaws the most tender and sensible part of a person. It is the principal part of hell's horror. A person may be relieved from bodily pains by proper medicines, but only the blood of Christ can relieve a troubled conscience.

*Lesson 3*

Hell is a dreadful place, where this cry is heard forever: "I thirst!" The wrath of the great and terrible God flames upon the damned forever. If Christ complained, "I thirst," when He had struggled but a few hours with God's wrath, what is the state of those who will grapple with it forever? When millions of years have gone, millions of years are still to come. There is an everlasting thirst in hell, and it admits no relief. Those who wallow in lavish and sensual pleasures must think on this. They must remember what Dives said: "Father Abraham, have mercy on me, and send Lazarus, that he may dip the tip of his finger in water, and cool my tongue; for I am tormented in this flame" (Luke 16:24). There are no cups of water in hell. If thirst in this life is so insufferable, what will infinitely greater thirst be like in eternity? We dare not think that God is harsh for treating sinners this way. We need to remember how He treated His dear Son when our sin was imputed to Him. If people refuse this precious Savior, then they have merited hell.

In Christ's thirst, we have the liveliest representation of the state of the damned. Here we see a person, laboring in extremity, under the infinite wrath of the great and terrible God, lying upon His soul and body, causing Him to utter this miserable cry: "I thirst!" Christ endured this for a little while, but the damned must endure it forever. Surely, this will be the cry of those who are cast away forever. O terrible thirst!

*Lesson 4*

Christ thirsted upon the cross; thus, believers will never thirst. There is a threefold thirst. The first is *natural*. It is a desire for refreshment by means of water. The second is *gracious*. It is the heart's vehement desire for God. "As the hart panteth after the water brooks, so panteth my soul after thee, O God. My soul thirsteth for God, for the living God: when shall I come and appear before God?" (Ps. 42:1–2). This is indeed a vehement thirst, and it makes the soul break with longings for God. It is proper to believers who have tasted that the Lord is gracious. The third is *penal*. It is God's just denial of relief to sinners in their extremity as a due punishment for their sin. Believers will never feel this kind of thirst, because Christ thirsted upon the cross, thereby making full satisfaction to God in our place. Christ's suffering was ordained for us and imputed to us.

Natural thirst will be satisfied in heaven. We will live without any dependence upon the creature. We will be equal with the angels in the way and manner of living and subsisting (Luke 20:36). Gracious thirst will also be satisfied in heaven. "Blessed are they which do hunger and thirst after righteousness: for they shall be filled" (Matt. 5:6). We will no longer depend upon the stream, because we will drink from the overflowing fountain itself (Ps. 36:8). All our thirsty desires will be filled with complete satisfaction. O how desirable a state is heaven! We should be restless until we get there. This present state is one of thirsting; the future state is one of refreshment and satisfaction. At present, some drops indeed come from the fountain by faith, but they do not quench the believer's thirst. Rather, like water sprinkled on the fire, they make it burn the more.

O bless God that Christ thirsted under the heat of His wrath so that we might never be scorched by it! If He had not cried, "I thirst," we would eternally cry of thirst and never be satisfied.

## Lesson 5

God's love for sinners is beyond all comparison. Three considerations marvelously heighten His love. First, He put Christ into this miserable condition. None of us could endure to see our own child in such torment. We would not do it for the greatest inheritance on earth. But such was the strength of God's love for us that He willingly gave up Christ to all this misery and torture for us. What should we call this love? What is "the breadth, and length, and depth, and height" of that love (Eph. 3:18)? It "passeth knowledge" (v. 19). The love of God to Christ was infinitely beyond all the love we have for our children, as the sea is more than a spoonful of water. And yet, as dearly as He loved Him, He was content to expose Him to all this so that we should not perish eternally.

Second, the Father did not relieve Christ despite His cries and complaints. Christ's voice pierced heaven and reached the Father's ear, but He did not refresh Him or decrease any of the debt He was paying. All this was because of the love He has for poor sinners. If God had pitied and spared Christ in His suffering, then He could not have pitied or spared us. The extremity of Christ's suffering was an act of justice to Him and the greatest mercy to us. Indeed, though He so bitterly complains of His thirst, Christ was not willing to be relieved until He had finished His work. O unspeakable love! He does not complain so that He might be relieved, but to manifest the greatness of the sorrow that His soul felt on our account.

Third, it should never be forgotten that Christ was exposed to these extremities of sorrow for the greatest of sinners who did not deserve one drop of God's mercy. This commends the love of God to us, "in that, while we were yet sinners, Christ died for us" (Rom. 5:8). Thus, the love of God in Christ rises higher and higher in every discovery of it. Admire, adore, and be ravished with the thoughts of this love! Thanks be to God for His unspeakable gift!

# 13

# The Completion of Christ's Work

*When Jesus therefore had received the vinegar, he said, It is finished: and he bowed his head, and gave up the ghost.*
—JOHN 19:30

"It is finished." This is Christ's sixth statement while upon the cross. He uttered it as a triumphant shout when He saw the glorious result of all His suffering at hand. It is only one word in the original language, but that single word contains the sum of all joy.

Some expositors are of the opinion that the antecedent to this expression is the legal types and ceremonies of the Old Testament. And so, when Christ says, "It is finished," He means that all the types that foreshadowed His work of redemption are now fulfilled and accomplished. Without doubt, this is implied in Christ's declaration, but it is not the principal sense. A far greater truth is contained in these words—namely, Christ's completion of the whole design and project of our redemption. It must be observed that when we say that Christ finished His work of redemption by His death, we do not mean that His death alone finished it, for His resurrection and ascension had a part in it. But these were to follow so soon after His death that they are included in the scope of His declaration. "By one offering he hath perfected for ever them that are sanctified" (Heb. 10:14).

*Doctrine: Christ has completely finished the great work of redemption, committed to Him by the Father.*

"I have glorified thee on the earth: I have finished the work which thou gavest me to do" (John 17:4). What was the work that Christ finished by His death? It was the fulfilling the whole law of God on our behalf (as our surety) for our redemption. The law is a glorious thing. The jealousy of the Lord watched over every point of it, for His dreadful and glorious name was upon it. "Cursed is every one that continueth not in all things which are written in the book of the law to do them" (Gal. 3:10). Two things, therefore, were required in Christ in order for Him to fulfill it. First, there must be a *subjective* perfection. Without this, He could never say, "It is finished." Perfect working always follows a perfect being. Therefore, in order to finish this great work of obedience, He must be holy (Luke 1:35). "For such an high priest became us, who is holy, harmless, undefiled, separate from sinners, and made higher than the heavens" (Heb. 7:26). Second, there must be an *effective* perfection. This is a perfection of working and obeying. Christ possessed this, for He continued in all things written in the law to do them. He fulfilled all righteousness (Matt. 3:15). He did all that was required to be done and suffered all that was required to be suffered. He did and suffered all that was commanded or threatened, in such perfection of obedience, both active and passive, that the pure eye of divine justice could not find any flaw in it. And so He finished the work that His Father had given Him to do.

## The Nature of Christ's Work

First, it was a *necessary* work. This is true in three ways. (1) It was necessary on the Father's account. I do not mean that God was under any necessity from His nature to redeem us this way or any other way. Our redemption is an act of the free counsel of God. But when God had decreed and determined to redeem and save poor sinners by Christ, then it became necessary that God's counsel should be fulfilled (Acts 4:28). (2) It was necessary on Christ's account. He had made a covenant with His Father. "Truly the Son of man goeth, as it was determined" (Luke 22:22). He was, therefore, under the necessity of fulfilling His engagement to the Father (John 9:3). (3) It was necessary on our account. If Christ had not finished this work, sin would quickly have finished our lives, hopes, and comforts. Without the completion of this work, no one would ever have been able to see the face of God. "And as Moses lifted up the serpent in the wilderness, even so must the Son of man be lifted up: That whosoever believeth in him should not perish, but have eternal life" (John 3:14–15).

Second, it was a *difficult* work. It cost many cries, groans, and tears for Christ to say, "It is finished." All the angels in heaven could never lift that burden one inch from the ground, yet Christ bore it upon His shoulders. The weight of this burden is evident in His deep agony in the garden and in His bitter cry on the cross.

Third, it was a *precious* work. It was finished in a few hours, but it will be the matter of everlasting songs and celebrations to the angels and saints for all eternity. O it was a precious work! Great mercies now flow out of this fountain (e.g., justification, sanctification, and adoption). It is the source of the endless glory and happiness of the world to come. What shouts of triumphs should there be among the saints when we hear these words: "It is finished!"

### The Manner of Christ's Work

First, Christ *obediently* finished His work. He became obedient to death, "even the death of the cross" (Phil. 2:8). His obedience was the obedience of a servant, but it was not servile obedience. "The Lord GOD hath opened mine ear, and I was not rebellious, neither turned away back" (Isa. 50:5). He heartily submitted Himself to every burden.

Second, Christ *freely* finished His work. Freedom and obedience are not mutually exclusive. Moses' mother nursed him in obedience to the command of Pharaoh's daughter, yet she did it most freely. So it is true of Christ. "Therefore doth my Father love me, because I lay down my life, that I might take it again. No man taketh it from me, but I lay it down of myself. I have power to lay it down, and I have power to take it again. This commandment have I received of my Father" (John 10:17–18). He liked the work because of the end in view. When He came into the world, He gave full and free consent to His Father's calling: "Lo, I come…I delight to do thy will, O my God" (Ps. 40:7–8).

Third, Christ *diligently* finished His work. He worked hard from the beginning of His life to its end. He was never idle, but "went about doing good" (Acts 10:38). As the lives of some people are but a diversion from one trifle to another, and from one pleasure to another, so the whole life of Christ was taken up with one work or another. Every moment of His time was employed for God to finish this work.

Fourth, Christ *completely* finished His work. All that was to be done by way of meritorious redemption was fully done. Whatever the law demanded was perfectly paid, and whatever a sinner needs was perfectly obtained. Nothing can be added to what Christ has done. "It is finished."

### The Evidence That Christ's Work Is Finished

First, Christ's blood was of infinite value and efficacy, sufficiently able to accomplish all the ends for which it was shed. The effect (i.e., the meritorious completion of the work of redemption) does not exceed the power of the cause to which we assign it (e.g., the death of Christ). There was certainly enough in Christ's blood to satisfy the utmost demand of justice. When it was actually shed, justice was fully paid and, consequently, the people (for whom it is paid) are fully redeemed from the curse on account of its merit.

Second, God the Father raised Him from the dead and seated Him at His right hand. If Christ (the surety) is discharged by God (the creditor), then the debt is fully paid. At His resurrection, Christ was justified and cleared from all charges and demands of justice (1 Tim. 3:16). The surety (who was confined for our debt) was set at liberty. Christ says the same of His ascension: the Holy Spirit shall convince the world "of righteousness, because I go to my Father, and ye see me no more" (John 16:10). There is complete and perfect righteousness in Him, which can be imputed to sinners for their perfect justification. We can be sure because He has ascended to the Father. There is a great deal of weight in these words: "ye see me no more." It amounts to this: because Christ has gone to heaven, where He abides in glory with His Father, we are satisfied that He has fully and completely performed all righteousness by His active and passive obedience and that He has so fully satisfied God for us that we will never be condemned. His Father will not send Him back, for nothing has been omitted (Heb. 10:12–14).

Third, it is evident Christ has finished the work by its blessed effects upon all who believe in Him. By virtue of the completeness of Christ's work, our conscience is now rationally pacified, and our soul at death is actually received into glory. Neither of these could be if Christ had not finished His work. If Christ had done His work imperfectly, He could not have given rest to the burdened souls that come to Him (Matt. 11:28), for our conscience would still be hesitating and trembling. If He had not finished His work, He could not have become the entrance through the veil of His flesh into heaven (Heb. 10:19–20). If He had but almost done His work, we would be but almost saved—that is, certainly damned.

## Application

### Lesson 1

Christ has completely finished all His work for us. What a sweet relief! All our works are defective, and all our duties are imperfect. There is much vanity and impudence in our best efforts. But here is great relief: Christ has finished all His work, even though we finish none of ours. We are poor and imperfect creatures in ourselves, yet we are "complete in him" (Col. 2:10). We cannot perfectly obey or fulfill one command of the law, yet "the righteousness of the law" is fulfilled in us (Rom. 8:4). Christ's complete obedience, being imputed to us, makes us complete and without fault before God.

It is true that we ought to be humbled for our defects and troubled for our every failing in obedience. But we should not be discouraged, even if multitudes of weaknesses are upon us and mountains of infirmities surround us. Though we have no righteousness of our own, Christ is made unto us righteousness (1 Cor. 1:30). And His righteousness is infinitely better than our own. O blessed be God for Christ's perfect righteousness!

*Lesson 2*

Christ finished His work with His own hands. It is, therefore, dangerous and dishonorable to add anything to the righteousness of Christ in point of justification before God. Christ will not endure it, because it reflects dishonorably upon His work. He will be everything or nothing in our justification. If He has finished the work, what need could there be for additions? What purpose could they serve? Did He finish the work by Himself, and will He now divide the glory and praise with us? No. Christ is not half a savior. O it is a hard thing to bring proud hearts to live upon Christ for righteousness! Certainly, God takes the right way to humble proud nature by calling sinners from their own righteousness to Christ's for their justification.

*Lesson 3*

Christ finished His work for us; therefore, there is no doubt that He will finish His work in us. As He began and completed the work of redemption, so He will complete what He has started in us (Phil. 1:6). Christ is not only the author but the finisher of our faith (Heb. 12:2). If He begins it, there is no doubt He will finish it. Indeed, the completion of His work of redemption gives full evidence that He will also finish His work of sanctification in us. These two works are so related that the work He finished by His death, resurrection, and ascension would be pointless to us without the completion of His work of sanctification in us. As He presented a perfect sacrifice to God and finished His work of redemption, so He will present every believer perfect and complete. He will not lose the end of all His suffering. What purpose would His meritorious suffering serve without full and complete application? We should not be discouraged at the defects and imperfections of our inherent grace. We should be humbled for them but not dejected by them. As Christ finished His work of redemption for us, so too He will finish His work of sanctification in us.

*Lesson 4*
Christ's work of redemption is complete and finished. This makes the way of faith exceedingly comfortable. Surely the way of believing is the most excellent way in which a poor sinner can approach God, for it brings before Him a complete and perfect righteousness. This is most honorable to God and most comfortable to the person who draws near to God. O what a complete, finished, and perfect thing is the righteousness of Christ! The searching eye of the holy God cannot find the least flaw or defect in it. We can turn it every way and view it on every side. It is pure and perfect, containing whatever is necessary for the reconciling of an angry God and the pacifying of a distressed soul. That faith, which presents so

complete and excellent an atonement to Him, is pleasing to Him. For this reason, the acting of our faith upon Christ for righteousness, and the approaching of faith to God with such an acceptable present, is called the work of God (John 6:29). One act of faith pleases Him more than an entire life spent in trying to obey the law.

*Lesson 5*

In finishing His work, Christ completed all that God gave Him to do. It is necessary, therefore, for us to work diligently. Will Christ work and we play? Will a zealous Christ be reproached with idle and lazy followers? "Work out your own salvation with fear and trembling" (Phil. 2:12). There remains nothing of Christ's work for us to do, but there is other work for us to do. We must work as well as Christ, though not for the same ends as Christ did. He worked to satisfy the law by fulfilling all righteousness. He worked out a righteousness to justify us before God. This work falls to no one other than Christ. But we must work to obey Christ's commands, testify our thankfulness to Christ, and glorify God by our obedience (Matt. 5:16). For this reason, our life must be a working life. May God preserve all His people from the vile opinions of libertines and antinomians, who champion grace and disparage obedience! Under the pretense of exalting a naked Christ upon the throne, they indeed strip Him naked of a great part of His glory and thereby dethrone Him.

# 14

# Christ's Burial

*Then took they the body of Jesus, and wound it in linen
clothes with the spices, as the manner of the Jews is to
bury. Now in the place where he was crucified there was
a garden; and in the garden a new sepulchre, wherein
was never man yet laid. There laid they Jesus therefore
because of the Jews' preparation day; for the sepulchre
was nigh at hand.*

—JOHN 19:40–42

We have heard Christ's last words, commending His spirit
into His Father's hands. And now the life of the world hangs
dead upon a tree. The light of the world hangs hidden in a
dreary cloud. The Sun of Righteousness enters the shadow of
death. The Lord is dead. We now come to His burial. "Come,
see the place where the Lord lay" (Matt. 28:6). There are three
remarkable particulars in our verse.

First, the *preparation*: "Then took they the body of Jesus,
and wound it in linen clothes with the spices." Christ's body
could not be buried until His friends had obtained it from His
judge. It was by law under Pilate's power and authority. When
they received it from Pilate, they "wound it in linen clothes

with the spices." In this way, they manifested their deep affection for Christ.

Second, the *grave*: "there was a garden; and in the garden a new sepulchre, wherein was never man yet laid." Two things are noteworthy about this tomb. First, it belonged to someone else. As Christ lived in other men's houses, so He lay in another man's tomb. Second, it was new. Here we see the wonderful providence of God. If someone else had been buried there, it might have discredited the glory of Christ's resurrection by casting doubt as to which body emerged from the tomb.

Third, the *burial*: "There laid they Jesus therefore because of the Jews' preparation day." Given the restrictions of time, His body was placed in the tomb with great solemnity. There was no pomp or ceremony. There were no external marks of honor. Thus, He was laid in His grave, where He continued for three incomplete days and nights in the land of darkness and forgetfulness.

*Doctrine: Christ's dead body was buried by several of His disciples and continued in that state for a time.*

### The Need for Christ's Burial

Why is Christ's burial important? First, it was necessary to establish the certainty of His death. In the Jews' kind of embalming, Christ's mouth, ears, and nostrils were filled with spices, and He was bound in linen. He was then laid long enough in the tomb to remove all doubt as to the certainty of His death. Second, it was necessary for Christ to fulfill the Old Testament types and prophecies. Christ's abode in the grave was prefigured by Jonah's abode three days and nights in the belly of the whale (Matt. 12:40). Long before Christ was born, the prophet spoke of the tomb in which His body would be laid (Isa. 53:9). Third, it was necessary for Christ to complete His humiliation. His burial was the lowest step He could possibly take in His abased state. He came to the dust of the earth. Fourth, it was necessary for Christ to conquer death in its own dominion. This victory furnished the saints with a triumphant song of deliverance: "O death, where is thy sting? O grave, where is thy victory?" (1 Cor. 15:55). Our graves would not be so comfortable to us if Christ had not been there before us and for us. Death is a dragon, and the grave is its den—a place of dread and terror. But Christ enters the den, overcomes the dragon, and disarms it of its terror. Death has become exceedingly beneficial to the saints—a bed of rest.

**The Nature of Christ's Burial**

Christ's burial was humble in that there was no external pomp. Humiliation marked His life, death, and burial. Yet it was accompanied by several miracles. First, there was an extraordinary eclipse of the sun. It fainted at the sight of such a sorry spectacle and clothed the heavens in black. Second, the earth shook. This was a sign of God's fierce indignation (Nah. 1:6). It revealed the greatness of His power and showed the people what they deserved and what He could do to them. It served to convince the world that it was indeed the Son of God who died. Third, the temple curtain was torn in two. This served to confirm that the Old Testament ceremonies were accomplished and abolished and that believers now enjoy free access into heaven. Fourth, the graves were opened. This showed the purpose of Christ's descending into the grave. It no longer has dominion over the bodies of the saints but has been vanquished and destroyed by Christ. This was further confirmed by those saints who arose from the grave and appeared to many in Jerusalem.

What will we say of Christ as He lay in the grave? He is a Sun of Righteousness, fountain of life, and bundle of love. Here lies Christ, in whom is treasured up all that an angry God requires for His satisfaction and all that an empty person requires for his perfection.

### Application

*Lesson 1*

We see the depth of Christ's humiliation for us. It was not enough that He (who was in the form of God) became a poor man, to spend His days in poverty and contempt. But He also became a dead corpse for our sakes. O what manner of love is this! It shows us the heinousness of sin in that it deserves such humiliation. It also shows us the fullness of Christ's satisfaction, whereby He closes the breach between God and us. O it was deep humiliation indeed! Does He look like the Son of God, whom all the angels adore? He is carried from Golgotha to the grave, and there He lies as a captive to death. There has never been such humiliation in the whole world.

*Lesson 2*

Christ's burial produces the strongest encouragement for believers against the fear of death. Christ lay in the grave for us. We do not need to fear the grave, for God will be with us, and He will surely bring us up from there. The consideration that Christ has been in the grave imparts manifold encouragements to the people of God against the terrors of the grave.

First, the grave could not destroy Christ. Death swallowed Him, as the whale swallowed Jonah, but it could not digest Him. It quickly delivered Him up again. Christ's lying in the grave as the common head and representative of believers is a great comfort. As it fared with Christ's physical body, so it will fare with His mystical body. It could not retain Him; therefore, it will not retain us. The resurrection of Christ out of His grave is the very ground of our hope for a resurrection out of our graves (1 Cor. 15:20).

Second, the union between the body of Christ and the divine nature was not dissolved in the grave. Similarly, the union between Christ and believers can never be dissolved, not even when our bodies are placed in the grave. It is true that the natural union between Christ's soul and body was dissolved for a time, but the hypostatical union was never dissolved. His body was still the body of the Son of God when it was in the grave. In like manner, the natural union between our souls and bodies is dissolved by death, but the mystical union between Christ and us (yea, between Christ and our dust) can never be dissolved.

Third, Christ's body, while in the grave, rested in hope and was assuredly a partaker of that hope. So it will fare with the dead bodies of the saints when they lie down in the dust. "My flesh also shall rest in hope" (Ps. 16:9–11). In like manner we commit our bodies to the dust in hope (Prov. 14:32). As Christ's hope was not in vain, neither is our hope in vain.

Fourth, Christ's lying in the grave has completely altered the nature of the grave. It is no longer what it once was. It was a part of the curse (Gen. 3:19). The grave served as a prison to keep the bodies of sinners until the great judgment. Now, for believers, it is no longer a prison but a bed of rest. "He shall enter into peace: they shall rest in their beds" (Isa. 57:2). O, then, let not believers stand in fear of the grave. Those who have one foot in heaven do not need to fear to put the other foot in the grave. "Though I walk through the valley of the shadow of death, I will fear no evil: for thou art with me" (Ps. 23:4).

Indeed, the grave is a terrible place to those who are outside of Christ. Death is God's police officer to arrest them. The grave is His prison to hold them. When death draws them into the grave, it draws them (as a lion does its prey) into the den to devour them (Ps. 49:14). Death reigns over them in its full power (Rom. 5:14). Although it will finally surrender them to God on the day of judgment, it would be better for them to lie forever where they are. On that day, they will be brought out of their graves as condemned prisoners out of the prison, to go to execution. But this is not the case with the saints. The grave (thanks be to our Lord Jesus Christ) is a privileged place while we sleep there. When we awake, it will be with singing. When we awake, we will be satisfied with His likeness.

## Lesson 3

Christ's people reap many privileges from His lying in the grave. If we expect rest and comfort in our graves, we must be in union with Christ now. If Christ is ours, we carry to our graves that which is better than all the gold and silver in the world. If we die in the Lord (i.e., interested in and united to the Lord), we take all grounds of comfort with us to our graves.

First, God's covenant holds firm during the body's appointed time in the grave. "I am the God of Abraham, and the God of Isaac, and the God of Jacob[.] God is not the God of the dead, but of the living" (Matt. 22:32). Abraham, Isaac, and Jacob are naturally dead. But God, long after their deaths, proclaimed Himself to be their God, thereby indicating that they are alive. Their covenant relationship with Him still lives. "Whether we live, we live unto the Lord; and whether we die, we die unto the Lord: whether we live therefore, or die, we are the Lord's" (Rom. 14:8). What an encouragement is this! We are as much the Lord's in the state of the dead as we are in the state of the living. Death puts an end to all other relationships, but the bond of the covenant dies not in the grave. Our dust is still the Lord's.

Second, God's love for our very dust is unchangeable. "I am the God of Abraham." God looks down from heaven into the graves of His saints with delight and on that pile of dust with satisfaction. Death does not separate us from God's love (Rom. 8:38–39). It was not our natural beauty that drew God's love to us; thus, He will not cease to love us when that beauty is gone. The goldsmith does not value the dust of his gold as much as God values the dust of His saints, for all their precious particles are united to Christ.

Third, God's providence will determine when our graves are to be prepared. He will not dig them until we are fit to be put into them. He will bring us to our graves at the best time. It is said of David that "after he had served his own generation by the will of God, fell on sleep" (Acts 13:36). It is the holy and wise will of God that orders our death.

Fourth, God's pardon has loosed all the bonds of guilt from us so that we will not die in our sins. What a comfort is this! We are the Lord's freemen in the grave. Sin threatens us: "Ye shall die in your sins" (John 8:24). It is better to be cast alive into a pit among snakes than to be cast dead into our graves among our sins. Here is a terrible warning: "His bones are full of the sin of his youth, which shall lie down with him in the dust" (Job 20:11). But all the saints are delivered from the company of their sins in the grave. God's free and final pardon has shut guilt out of our graves.

Fifth, Christ has slain the enmity of the grave. Now it has become a privileged place for us. For this reason, the apostle says, "Death is yours" (see 1 Cor. 3:21–22)—that is, "yours" as a friend or privilege. It is there that we find sweet rest in Christ.

Sixth, Christ keeps the keys of all the chambers of death. As He unlocks the door of death when He lets us in, so He will open it when we awake to let us out. From the time He opens it to let us in until the time He opens it to let us out, He watches by us while we sleep. "I…have the keys of hell and of death" (Rev. 1:18). If we expect peace and rest in the chambers of death, we must make sure we are in union with Christ. A grave with Christ is a comfortable place.

# 15

# The Blessed Ends of Christ's Humiliation

*He shall see of the travail of his soul, and shall be satisfied.*
—ISAIAH 53:11

It is unimaginable that Christ should so abase Himself by stooping from the bosom of His Father to the state of the dead without some glorious purpose in view. This is precisely what we read in this verse: "He shall see the travail of his soul, and shall be satisfied." The expression "travail of his soul" refers to the agonies of His soul and torments of His body, not only because of their sharpness and acuteness but because they make way for the birth that abundantly rewards all His labors. Christ understood what it would mean to enjoy the fruition of His suffering. He did not shed His blood for nothing. His design does not miscarry. He certainly accomplishes the ends at which He aimed, and this brings Him great satisfaction. "A woman when she is in travail hath sorrow, because her hour is come: but as soon as she is delivered of the child, she remembereth no more the anguish, for joy that a man is born into the world" (John 16:21). When God finished His work of creation, He viewed it with pleasure and satisfaction. Likewise, our exalted Redeemer is satisfied with the happy result of His hard suffering.

*Doctrine: Christ will certainly attain all the blessed ends for which He humbled Himself to death.*

Let us inquire into the ends of Christ's humiliation. As the sprinkling of blood in the Old Testament was done for weighty ends, so too Christ's precious blood was shed for weighty ends.

**To Deliver from Danger**

In the Old Testament, blood was shed to deliver from danger (Ex. 12:13). Likewise, Christ shed His blood to deliver His people from danger—namely, the wrath that burns to the lowest hell. Christ "delivered us from the wrath to come" (1 Thess. 1:10). The expression "wrath to come" implies that this wrath is future and perpetual. It will certainly and inevitably come upon sinners. As sure as the night follows the day, and as sure as the winter follows the summer, so wrath will follow sin. When it comes, it will abide. When millions of years are gone, it will still be "wrath to come." By His death, Christ has delivered His people from this wrath. "Being now justified by his blood, we shall be saved from wrath through him" (Rom. 5:9). Christ's blood was the price that ransomed us from God's wrath.

First, Christ has delivered us *freely*. He voluntarily assumed His mediatorial office, and He was moved to do so by His tender compassion toward His elect. We were at one time a lost generation. We had sold ourselves and our inheritance into slavery, and we did not have the means to redeem either. But our kinsman, to whom the right of redemption belonged, undertook to redeem us and our inheritance (Eph. 1:10; 1 Peter 1:4). He did it freely, before any supplication was made to Him. He designed it freely, before we even existed. When the purpose of His grace came to its fullness, He freely poured out the infinite treasure of His blood to purchase our deliverance from wrath.

Second, Christ has delivered us *fully*. It is full in respect of time. It was not merely a reprieve, but a deliverance. He did not shed His blood to delay our execution for a while, but to procure our eternal deliverance from wrath. Therefore, "he became the author of eternal salvation unto all them that obey him" (Heb. 5:9). As it is full in respect of time, so it is full in respect of degrees. He did not die to procure a reduction to the severity of the sentence, but to rescue His people fully from all degrees of wrath. There is no condemnation to those who are in Christ (Rom. 8:1). Every drop of God's wrath was poured into the bitter cup that Christ drank.

Third, Christ has delivered us *uniquely*. It is not common to all, but peculiar to some. By nature, we are no better than those who are left under God's wrath. As to natural disposition, moral qualifications, and external endowments, oftentimes we are far inferior to those who perish. How often do we find moral righteousness, innocence, resourcefulness, and readiness to all offices of love in those who are under the dominion of other lusts and under the damning sentence of the law? Meanwhile, proud, peevish, sensual, and unpolished natures are chosen to be the subjects of this salvation (1 Cor. 1:26).

Fourth, Christ has delivered us *wonderfully*. It would weary an angel to write down all the wonders that are in this salvation. Christ took our nature and suffered the penalty of the law. He secured our deliverance when He and His design seemed to be lost. These are wonders that will take eternity to search, admire, and adore.

### To Atone for Sin

In the Old Testament, blood was shed and sprinkled to make atonement between God and the people (Lev. 4:20). Its efficacy stood in its relation to Christ's blood, which it signified and shadowed. Hence, the people were reconciled to God by the expiation and remission of their sins. What was shadowed in this typical blood was really accomplished by Christ in the shedding of His blood.

Reconciliation of the elect to God is, therefore, another one of those beautiful works for which Christ travailed (Rom. 5:10). It was God's principal design in Christ's humiliation (2 Cor. 5:18–19; Col. 1:20). God filled Christ with grace and authority. The Spirit of God was in Him to qualify Him. The authority of God was in Him by commission to validate all that He did. The love of God for humanity was in Him. One of the principal effects in which this love was manifested was the purpose for which He came—to reconcile the world to God. For this reason, Christ is called the "propitiation for our sins" (1 John 2:2). Now, atonement is nothing else but the healing of the ancient friendship between God and people and to bring these enemies into a state of sweet concord. The means by which this blessed design was effectually accomplished was Christ's death, which made complete satisfaction to God for the wrong we had done Him. The following particulars are noteworthy.

First, this reconciliation is secured by Christ's death because it satisfies God's justice. When reparation is made, enmity ceases. "The chastisement of our peace was upon him; and with his stripes we are healed" (Isa. 53:5). By His "chastisement" Christ removed our sins and procured our peace. The guilt of our sin was discharged with the price of His blood. This reconciliation is made and continued between God and us by (1) the oblation of Christ for us whereby we are meritoriously reconciled, (2) the application of Christ and His benefits to us (through faith) whereby we are actually reconciled, and (3) the continuation of Christ's sacrifice in heaven, through His eternal intercession, whereby our state of reconciliation is confirmed and all breaches prevented. If Christ had not died, His death could never be applied to us nor pleaded for us in heaven. When we were enemies, we were reconciled to God by the death of His Son (Rom. 5:10)—that is, Christ's death meritoriously (or virtually) reconciled us to God. It is the application of Christ to us by faith that makes the meritorious reconciliation become actual reconciliation (Eph. 2:16–17). This state of friendship is continued by Christ's intercession within the veil, so that there can never be any breaches made to our peace (1 John 2:1–2).

Second, this reconciliation could only be made by Christ's death. Only He who was God manifested in our flesh could offer a sacrifice of sufficient value to make amends to God for the wrong done to Him by sin. How could God readmit us into favor without full satisfaction? He is indeed inclined to acts of mercy, but we must never suppose that

He exercises one attribute to the prejudice of another. Is His justice eclipsed so that His mercy might shine? It cannot be thought possible. Christ's death, therefore, was the most just, effectual, and honorable way to make up the peace between God and us.

Third, this reconciliation is offered to us by the gospel upon certain conditions. Unless we fulfill these, notwithstanding all that Christ has done and suffered, the breach still continues between God and us. It is His grace that brings us to those terms of reconciliation. And, surely, He has not suspended the mercy of our reconciliation upon unreasonable conditions. The two grand articles of peace with God are repentance and faith. In the first, we lay down our arms against God. In the second, we accept Christ and His pardon with a thankful heart, yielding ourselves to His government. These are the terms on which we are actually reconciled to God (Rom. 5:1). Surely it would not become the holy God to own as His friend and favorite someone who goes on perversely and impenitently in the way of sin, or to receive into friendship someone who slights and rejects Christ, whose precious blood was shed to procure and purchase peace and pardon for sinners. But if there is any poor sinner who says in his heart, "I repent of sinning against God," and is sincerely willing to come to Christ upon His terms, he will have peace.

Fourth, this reconciliation is not a common peace. It puts the reconciled person beyond all possibility of ever again coming under God's wrath (Isa. 54:10). Christ is a surety to prevent new breaches (2 John 2). This is the fountain from which all other comforts flow to us. As trade flourishes and riches abound when peace is made between states and kingdoms, so all spiritual and temporal mercies flow into our hearts once we are reconciled to God. This is a great comfort in a day of straits and dangers and in a dying day. We cannot fully declare it, for it passes all understanding (Phil. 4:7).

**To Cleanse from Pollution**
In the Old Testament, blood was shed to purify people from their ceremonial pollution (Lev. 14:6–7). Typical blood was shed to purify those who were unclean, and so was the blood of Christ shed to purge away the sins of His people (Eph. 5:25–26). "And for their sakes I sanctify myself" (John 17:19)—that is, He devoted Himself to death that we might be sanctified through the truth. This is the substance of the Lamb's song in heaven: "Unto him that loved us, and washed us from our sins in his own blood…to him be glory and dominion for ever and ever" (Rev. 1:5–6).

There is a twofold evil in sin: guilt and pollution. Justification cures the former and sanctification the latter. Both justification and sanctification flow to sinners out of Christ's death. And though it is proper to say that the Holy Spirit sanctifies, it is certain that it was Christ's blood that procured for us the Spirit of sanctification. If Christ had not died, the Holy Spirit would never have come down from heaven for any such purpose. It was the pouring forth of Christ's blood for us that obtained the pouring forth of the Spirit of holiness upon us. Therefore, it is said that Christ "came by water and blood" (1 John 5:6)—water to purify from filth and blood to wash away guilt.

This fruit of Christ's death, even our sanctification, is an incomparable mercy. Why? First, holiness is the soul's highest beauty, because it is the image and glory of God (Ex. 15:11; Col. 3:10). When the guilt and filth of sin are washed away, the beauty of God is put upon the soul in sanctification. It is a beam of divine glory upon the creature, enamoring the very heart of Christ. Second, holiness is the soul's best evidence for heaven. "Blessed are the pure in heart: for they shall see God" (Matt. 5:8). "And holiness, without which no man shall see the Lord" (Heb. 12:14). No gifts, duties, or endowments will evidence a right to heaven, but the least measure of true holiness will secure heaven to the soul. Third, holiness is a continual source of comfort to those on the way to heaven. The purest and sweetest pleasures in this world are the results of holiness. Until we come to live holy lives, we never live comfortable lives. Fourth, holiness is the peculiar mark by which God has visibly distinguished His own from other people. "The LORD hath set apart him that is godly for himself" (Ps. 4:3). He intends to do good to them forever.

### To Confirm the New Covenant

In the Old Testament, blood was shed to confirm God's covenant (Ex. 24:8). Christ has done the same with His blood. "This is my blood of the new testament" (Matt. 26:28). He means that it is ratified and confirmed by His blood. Where there is a testament, there must also of necessity be the death of the testator (Heb. 9:16). All the blessings and benefits bequeathed to believers in the last will and testament of Christ are abundantly confirmed and secured to them by His death. He died on purpose to make that testament of force to them. What is bequeathed to us in Christ's testament is altogether a free and voluntary donation. Christ gives us three sorts of goods.

First, He gives us all temporal good things (Matt. 6:33; 1 Tim. 6:17). By this I mean He gives us the comfort and blessing of all things, though not necessarily the possession of them (2 Cor. 6:10).

Second, He gives us all spiritual good things: justification (Rom. 3:24–26), sanctification (1 Cor. 1:30), adoption (Gal. 3:26), the ministry of angels (Heb. 1:14), and interest in all the promises (2 Peter 1:4). Thus, all spiritual good things that are in Christ's testament are conveyed to us.

Third, He gives us all eternal good things: heaven, glory, and eternal life (Rom. 8:10–11). Nothing like this was ever found in the testaments of princes. Those things that kings leave to their heirs are but trifles in comparison to what Christ has conferred in the New Testament upon His people. And all this is confirmed and ratified by His death, so that the promise is sure.

How Christ's death confirmed the New Testament is worth our inquiry. Christ died not only to confirm it by His blood, but His death ratified it as the death of a testator, which makes it irrevocable. When a person dies, his will is immediately in force. It can never be recalled. It is certain that the last will and testament of Christ is most sacred, and God will never annul it. Moreover, it is not with Christ as with other testators who must trust the performance of their wills to their executors. As Christ died to put it in force, so He lives again to be the executor of His own testament. All power to fulfill His will is now in His hands (Rev. 1:18).

## Application

*Lesson 1*

By His death, Christ has delivered His people from wrath. It is ungrateful for us to complain of the light afflictions we suffer upon His account in this world. Are these sufferings anything like those that our Redeemer suffered for us? Have any of us ever endured for Him what He endured for us? Is there anything in this world that we can suffer that compares to the "wrath to come"? (1) What is the wrath of man compared to the wrath of God? (2) What are the sufferings of the body compared to the tortures of the soul and body in hell? (3) What are the troubles of the present compared to that wrath which, after millions of years, will still be called "wrath to come"? (4) What comparison is there between the intermitting sorrows and sufferings of this life and the uninterrupted "wrath to come"? (5) How much more comfortable is it to suffer in fellowship with Christ and His saints for the sake of righteousness than to suffer with devils and reprobates on account of wickedness?

*Lesson 2*

Christ has delivered His people from wrath; therefore, there is little comfort in present earthly enjoyments until we know for certain that we are included in that deliverance. Present ease affords little comfort while hints of "wrath to come" daily disturb the conscience. The pleasures and enjoyments of the wicked feed them for the day of slaughter, but they have little appeal to those who understand their end. We must not rest until we have solid evidence that we are numbered among those whom Christ has delivered from "wrath to come." We can be satisfied as to the evidence in the following three ways.

First, we will forsake sin: "Thou shalt call his name JESUS: for he shall save his people from their sins" (Matt. 1:21). While people live under the guilt and dominion of sin, they lie exposed to "wrath to come." But when they are delivered from the guilt and power of sin, they are delivered from the danger of wrath. Where sin is not imputed, wrath is not threatened.

Second, we will esteem Christ: "Giving thanks unto the Father...who hath delivered us from the power of darkness, and hath translated us into the kingdom of his dear Son" (Col. 1:12–13). Christ is "dear" beyond all comparison to His saved ones. This is the natural effect of mercy upon those who have felt it.

Third, we will please Christ: "That ye might walk worthy of the Lord unto all pleasing, being fruitful in every good work, and increasing in the knowledge of God; Strengthened with all might, according to his glorious power, unto all patience and longsuffering with joyfulness" (Col. 1:10–11). There is a cheerful readiness to endure anything for Christ.

*Lesson 3*

It is a sad state to be excluded from the articles of peace with God. The impenitent unbeliever is not reconciled to God. He has an almighty enemy whose very frown is destruction (Deut. 32:40–42). He has an inescapable enemy whose hand reaches to the utmost parts of the earth (Ps. 139:10). He has an immortal enemy who lives forever to avenge Himself upon His adversaries. What will you do when you are in Saul's case? "Wherefore then dost thou ask of me, seeing the LORD is departed from thee, and is become thine enemy?" (1 Sam. 28:16). Where will you turn and what will you do when you see God, who is your enemy, upon the throne? Sad indeed is the case of all those who are not comprehended in the articles of peace with God.

*Lesson 4*

It is imperative that we give due diligence to clear up our interest in this reconciliation. If it was worth Christ's blood to purchase it, then it is worth our care to confirm it. And what better evidence is there than our conscientious tenderness of sin? If we are reconciled to God, we will say, "And now our God, seeing thou hast given us such a deliverance as this; should we again break thy commandments?" (see Ezra 9:13–14). If we are reconciled to God, His friends will be our friends, and His enemies will be our enemies. If God is our friend, we will be diligent to please Him (John 15:10, 14). Those who refuse to make peace with God are enemies to their own souls. And those who make peace but take no pains to confirm it are enemies to their own comfort.

*Lesson 5*

Christ died to sanctify His people. This shows us the Savior's love. He "loved us, and washed us from our sins in his own blood" (Rev. 1:5). He did not shed the blood of beasts, as the priests of old did, but His own blood (Heb. 9:12). His blood was precious (1 Peter 1:19), for it was the blood of God. One drop is greater than all the blood that runs in the veins of Adam's posterity. Christ bled every vein dry for us so that He bestowed the whole treasure of His blood upon us. And He did this when we were enemies. O what manner of love is this!

*Lesson 6*

Christ died to confirm the New Testament, in which He bestows wonderful legacies on believers. It concerns us, therefore, to ensure our title to the mercies contained in this blessed testament. We must do so in two ways.

First, we must examine our covenant relation to Christ. Are we His spouse? Have we forsaken all for Him (Ps. 45:10)? Are we ready to take our lot with Him in prosperity or adversity? Are we loyal to Him (Hos. 3:3)? Do we yield obedience to Him as our head and husband (Eph. 5:24)? If so, then we may be confident that we are interested in the benefits and blessings of Christ's last will and testament. He cannot make a testament and forget His spouse. If He so loved the church as to give Himself for her, He will bestow all that He has on her. Are we His children by regeneration? Are we born of the Holy Spirit? Do we resemble Christ in holiness (1 Peter 1:14–15)? Do we find a reverential fear of Christ leading us to obey Him in all things (Mal. 1:6)? Are we led by the Holy Spirit (Rom. 8:14)? Do we possess the spirit of adoption, enabling us to cry, "Abba, Father" (Gal. 4:6)? If so, we are His children. And if we are His children, we can be sure we have a rich legacy in Christ's last will and testament.

Second, we must examine the new covenant impressions that are made on our hearts. These include spiritual illumination (Jer. 31:34), tenderness of heart (Ezek. 11:19), and fear of God (Jer. 32:40). These things confirm that we are the children of the covenant—the people on whom all these great things are settled.

*Lesson 7*

As the recipients of such mercies, it is our duty to admire God's love and walk answerably to it. First, we must admire the love of Christ. O how intense and ardent was His love that He designed this great inheritance for us! Moreover, it was the travail of His soul. We should fall down astonished before this love, humbly professing that we owe ourselves (and all we are) to it. Second, we must be sure we walk in a way that is becoming of those for whom Christ has done such great things. We comfort ourselves under present afflictions with our spiritual privileges (James 2:5). All our joy should be in Christ and what we have in Him.

# 16

# Christ's Exaltation

*For if he were on earth, he should not be a priest.*
—HEBREWS 8:4

We have finished our consideration of Christ's humiliation and all that He accomplished by it. We now proceed to His exaltation, which advances and perfects His work of redemption. Christ's work was not finished on earth in His state of suffering and affliction. His exaltation was necessary for the completion of His work. From our verse, we learn that it is such a necessary part of His priesthood that, without it, He could not have been a priest. If He had remained on earth (that is, if He had not been raised from the dead and taken up to glory), He could not have been a complete and perfect priest.

In the Old Testament, it was not enough to kill the sacrifice thereby shedding its blood. After this was done, the blood had to be carried through the veil into the most holy place before the Lord (Heb. 9:7). So the shedding of Christ's blood on earth would not have been enough unless He had carried it into heaven and there performed His work of intercession for us.

In addition to this, God the Father stood engaged in a solemn covenant to reward Christ for His deep humiliation with a most glorious advancement (Isa. 49:5–7; Phil. 2:9). Justice required it should be so. How could our surety be detained in the prison of the grave, having fully discharged the debt for which He was imprisoned? The law of God must acknowledge itself to be fully satisfied in all its claims and demands. Christ's resurrection from the dead was His discharge upon full payment.

God the Father lost nothing by this, for there was never a more glorious manifestation of the name of God in the world than that which was manifested in this work. Speaking of Christ's exaltation, the apostle writes, "And that every tongue should confess that Jesus Christ is Lord, to the glory of God the Father" (Phil. 2:11). The love of God for poor sinners is astonishingly displayed in Christ's exaltation. To show the delight that He took in our recovery, He has openly declared to the world that His exalting of Christ to glory was bestowed upon Him as a reward for His work of redemption: "Wherefore God also hath highly exalted him" (Phil. 2:9). Our English is too flat to convey the fullness of the original. It is a super-exaltation. Other translations render it "He hath multiplied his sublimity," "He hath heightened him with a height," or "He hath famously exalted him." In short, God cannot raise Christ any higher. This is a great argument for God's satisfaction and contentment in the recovery of poor sinners. For this reason, glory and honor will be ascribed to God the Father in heaven for all eternity.

Now, this extraordinary exaltation of Christ properly respects His human nature, which alone is capable of advancement. In respect to His divine nature, He never ceased to be the Most High. He was exalted as a common person and as the head of all believers—their representative in this as well as in His other works. In this way, God shows what He intends to do with His people after they have suffered a while. Whatever God the Father intends to do in us or for us, He has first done it to the person of our representative, Jesus Christ.

The Scriptures testify to this in relation to all the steps of Christ's exaltation. Christ emerged from the grave as a public person: "If ye then be risen with Christ" (Col. 3:1). We have communion and fellowship with Him in His resurrection. Christ also ascended into heaven as a public person. He "hath raised us up together, and made us sit together in heavenly places in Christ Jesus" (Eph. 2:6). He sits at God's right hand as a common person, and we sit there in our representative. When He comes to judge the world, the saints will come with Him (Zech. 14:5). As they will come with Christ from heaven, so they will sit on thrones with Him to judge (1 Cor. 6:2). All this honor is given to Christ as our representative.

This is a source of great comfort to God's people. "Wherefore he is able also to save them to the uttermost that come unto God by him, seeing he ever liveth to make intercession for them" (Heb. 7:25). Our head is in heaven; therefore, we are safe in this world. Since He lives, we cannot die (John 14:19). We must never think that Christ's wonderful advancement might cause Him to forget His people who groan here below under sin and misery. The disposition of His tender and faithful heart is not changed with His condition. He bears the same respect to us as when He dwelt among us. Indeed, He acts and lives above on our account (Heb. 7:25; 1 John 2:1–2).

Meditations on Christ's exaltation are seasonable and comfortable, especially when sickness wastes our body and withers its beauty and when God brings us to the dust of death. We must remember that our "vile body" will be conformed to Christ's glorious body (Phil. 3:21). As God has glorified and highly exalted His Son, so He will exalt us. We will not be equal in glory with Christ, for He is distinguished by His peculiar glory from all angels and saints, just as the sun is known by its excellent glory from the lesser stars. But we will be conformed to our glorious head, according to the proportion of members.

Having spoken of Christ's exalted state, casting some light upon it and engaging our attention to it, I will now briefly open it according to its steps: (1) His resurrection, (2) His ascension, (3) His session at the Father's right hand, and (4) His return in judgment.

# 17

# Christ's Resurrection

*He is not here: for he is risen, as he said. Come, see the*
*place where the Lord lay.*
                                        —MATTHEW 28:6

God never intended for the darling of His soul to be lost in
an obscure grave. Thus, an angel descended from heaven to
roll away the stone and (with it) the reproach of His death.
The angel proclaimed Christ's resurrection to the two Marys,
who were drawn to visit the grave on account of their love for
Him. The majesty attending Christ's resurrection was so great
that "the keepers did shake, and became as dead men" (v. 4).
To encourage them, the angel declared, "He is not here: for he
is risen, as he said. Come, see the place where the Lord lay."
In these words, we have a declaration and confirmation of
Christ's resurrection from the dead. First, there is a declara-
tion: "He is not here: for he is risen." This is where they placed
His body and this is where they expected to find His body.
But they were mistaken. "He is not here." To remove all doubt,
the angel stated it positively and affirmatively: "He is risen."
The term imports the active power by which Christ raised
Himself. It was the divine nature (or Godhead) of Christ that

revived and raised the manhood. Second, there is a confirmation: "Come, see the place where the Lord lay." The grave has lost its guest: it is now empty. Death has lost its prey: it received Him but it could not retain Him.

*Doctrine: By the power of His own Godhead, Christ rose from the dead, to the consternation of His enemies and the consolation of His people.*

Christ's resurrection from the dead is confirmed by many infallible proofs (Acts 1:3). We have testimonies from heaven and earth. From heaven, we have the testimony of angels. The angel tells the two Marys, "He is risen." From earth, we have the testimony of holy men who were eyewitnesses of this truth. Christ showed Himself to these men over a space of forty days after His resurrection (1 Cor. 15:6). These were holy men who confirmed their testimony with their blood. No point of religion is of more infallible certainty than this.

Blessed be God that it is so! If Christ is not risen, then the gospel is in vain, seeing as the full weight of our faith, hope, and salvation rests upon it (1 Cor. 15:14). If Christ is not risen, then the divinely inspired apostles are false witnesses, for they affirmed it to the death (v. 15). If Christ is not risen, then we are still in our sins (v. 17), for our justification is truly ascribed to Christ's resurrection (Rom. 4:25). While Christ was dying, and continued in the state of the dead, the price of our redemption was being paid. The payment was not complete until He rose again. If Christ is not risen, then the dead have perished (1 Cor. 15:17). Even those who died, believing in Christ, are lost eternally. If Christ is not risen, then all the types that prefigured His resurrection are meaningless (Ps. 16:10; Matt. 12:40; Luke 24:46; 1 Cor. 15:4). To conclude, if Christ is not risen, then He has not been installed in glory in heaven (Rom. 14:9).

There remains no doubt as to the certainty of Christ's resurrection. Blessed be God that it is a nail fastened in a sure place! I do not need to spend any more time confirming it. Instead, I want to open the nature and manner of His resurrection.

**The Nature of Christ's Resurrection**

First, Christ rose from the dead with great majesty. "And, behold, there was a great earthquake: for the angel of the Lord descended from heaven, and came and rolled back the stone from the door, and sat upon it. His countenance was like lightning, and his raiment white as snow: And for fear of him the keepers did shake, and became as dead men" (Matt. 28:2–4). Human infirmity was unable to bear such heavenly majesty. Human nature sank under it. This earthquake was a sign of triumph, given by Christ, that He had overcome death in its own dominion. When God fought for His people in the days of the judges, "the earth trembled, and the heavens dropped, the clouds also dropped water. The mountains melted from before the LORD" (Judg. 5:4–5). In like manner, Christ emerged from the grave with great splendor and majesty, as becoming a mighty conqueror.

Second, Christ's resurrection was attended with the resurrection of many saints (Matt. 27:52–53). This wonder was designed to adorn Christ's resurrection and to give a pledge of our future resurrection. This was a special resurrection of the saints, intended to show what God will one day do for all His saints. In the moment, it served to give testimony of Christ's resurrection from the dead. Many people saw these resurrected saints. It is pointless to inquire as to what they did and said. God has cast a veil of silence and secrecy over these things. We must content ourselves with the written Word and accept that "if they hear not Moses and the prophets, neither will they be persuaded, though one rose from the dead" (Luke 16:31).

Third, Christ rose from the dead by the power of His own Godhead. He quickened and raised Himself. It was by virtue of His resurrection that the saints (who accompanied Him) were also raised. It was not the angel, who rolled back the stone, who revived Him in the grave. Christ resumed His own life. "I have power to lay it down, and I have power to take it again" (John 10:18). He was "put to death in the flesh, but quickened by the Spirit" (1 Peter 3:18)—that is, by the power of His Godhead (or divine nature), which is here opposed to His human nature. "Through the eternal Spirit [he] offered himself without spot to God" (Heb. 9:14). The "eternal Spirit" is not the third person of the Trinity, but His eternal Godhead. If it were the third person of the Trinity, then Christ's offering of Himself could not be ascribed to Him as His own act. It is by this same "eternal Spirit" (Godhead) that He was raised from the grave (Rom. 1:4). If He had been raised by the power of the Father or the Holy Spirit alone, and not by His own power, then how could He be declared to be the Son of God by His resurrection? What would make Him any different from those who have been raised by God's power? His resurrection was marvelous because no one but Him has ever been raised by a self-quickening principle. Many dead saints arose with Him, but they did so by virtue of Christ's resurrection. For this reason, Christ declared, when He raised Lazarus from the dead, "I am the resurrection, and the life" (John 11:25)—that is, the principle of life and quickening by which the dead are raised.

Fourth, Christ is "the firstborn from the dead" (Col. 1:18). Though Lazarus and others were raised before Him, they were not raised by themselves, but by Him. It was by His virtue and power, not their own, that they emerged from their graves. And though they were raised to life, they died again. But Christ will never die again (Rom. 6:9). He was first in creating the universe and first in rising from the dead, so that He might have the preeminence in all things.

Fifth, Christ was raised as a public person. He is "the firstfruits of them that slept" (1 Cor. 15:20). Our resurrection is secured by Christ's resurrection, for the firstfruits both assures and sanctifies the whole harvest.

### The Manner of Christ's Resurrection

Christ rose as a public person, representing and comprehending all the elect, who are called the children of the resurrection (Eph. 2:6). As we died in Adam (who was a public person), so we are raised from death in Christ, who is the head and representative of all His elect seed. He is the firstborn and first begotten from the dead with respect to the whole number of the elect who are to be raised from the dead in their time. As the whole harvest follows the firstfruits, so the general resurrection of the saints to eternal life follows the resurrection of the firstborn from the dead. It will surely follow as an effect follows its proper cause. Now, Christ's resurrection has a threefold causality upon our resurrection.

First, Christ's resurrection is the *meritorious* cause of our resurrection. It completed His satisfaction and finished His payment, and so our justification is properly assigned to it (Rom. 4:25). His resurrection was the receiving of the acquittance—the canceling of the bond. If He had not risen, we would still be in our sins (1 Cor. 15:17). But the price was paid in His death, and the payment was finished in His resurrection. Now nothing stands in the way of our resurrection to eternal life.

Second, Christ's resurrection is the *efficient* cause of our resurrection. When the time comes for the saints to rise out of the dust, they will be raised by Christ, as their head, in whom is found the effective principle of their life. "Your life is hid with Christ in God" (Col. 3:3). Christ, our mystical head, being quickened, the Spirit of life, who is in Him, will be diffused through all His members to quicken them also in the morning of the resurrection. Hence, the warm animating dew of Christ's resurrection is to our bodies as the dew of the morning to withered plants (Isa. 26:19). For this reason, the apostle reasons forward from Christ's resurrection to ours, and back again from our resurrection to Christ's (Rom. 8:10–11; 1 Cor. 15:12–13). Though we are really united to Christ by the Holy Spirit, our bodies must die. Though our bodies must die, they will live again in the resurrection. They will do so by virtue of the Holy Spirit who dwells in us. He is the bond of our mystical union with Christ, our head. We will not be raised as others are, by a mere word of power, but by the Spirit of life dwelling in Christ, our head.

Third, Christ's resurrection is the *exemplary* cause of our resurrection. He is the first and best and, therefore, is the pattern and measure of all the rest. "Who shall change our vile body, that it may be fashioned like unto his glorious body" (Phil. 3:21). The conformity of our resurrection to Christ's stands in the following particulars.

First, Christ's body was raised substantially the same as it was before, and so will ours be. "This corruptible must put on incorruption, and this mortal must put on immortality" (1 Cor. 15:53). The apostle was (as it were) pointing to his own body when he spoke these words. It will be both who it was and what it was. To deny this is to deny the resurrection itself. If God were to prepare another body to be raised instead of this one, it would not be a resurrection but a creation.

Second, Christ's body was raised not by a word of power from the Father but by His own Spirit, and so will ours be. Indeed, God's power will go forth to raise sinners from the dead, but our resurrection will be effected in another way. We will be raised by Christ's Spirit who now dwells in us. The very Spirit of Christ, who effected our spiritual resurrection from sin, will effect our bodily resurrection from the grave.

Third, Christ's body was marvelously improved by His resurrection, and so will ours be. It fell in weakness but was raised in power, no longer capable of pains, sorrows, and dishonors. In like manner, the believer's body is "sown in dishonour" but "raised in glory," "sown in weakness" but "raised in power," "sown a natural body" but "raised a spiritual body" (1 Cor. 15:43–44). By "a spiritual body" the apostle does not mean properly but analogically. It is no longer subject to any of those natural necessities to which it is now tied. There are no flaws, defects, or deformities in the children of the resurrection. All bodily defects and deformities will be restored to perfect being and beauty. Our bodies will be free from the law of mortality (Luke 20:35–36).

Fourth, Christ's body was raised from the dead to be glorified and crowned with honor. It was a joyful day for Him, and so our resurrection will be a day of gladness. "Awake and sing, ye that dwell in dust" (Isa. 26:19). O how comfortable will be the meeting between the glorified soul and its new raised body! Three things will make it so. (1) It will be comfortable because of the gratification of the soul in the satisfaction of its natural appetite for union with its own body. Even glorified souls in heaven desire to be reunited with their bodies. At present, we are sensible of the soul's affection to the body. We feel its tender care for the body, its sympathy with it, and its unwillingness to be separated from it. "We are at home in the body" (2 Cor. 5:6). This inclination remains with the soul in heaven. It does not reckon itself to be completely happy until reunited with its dear companion and partner. When the soul's longing is satisfied with the enjoyment of the body again, what a comfortable meeting will it be! (2) It will be comfortable because of the excellent state in which the soul and body will meet. As the body will be raised with all the improvements and endowments imaginable, so the soul will descend immediately from God out of heaven, shining in its glory and holiness. And thus it reenters its body and animates it again. (3) It will be comfortable because the soul and body will together meet the Lord and be with Him forever. It will be a day of triumph and exaltation. What an ecstasy of joy and ravishing pleasure will it be for the soul to resume its own body and meet the Lord! Surely, it will be a joyful awakening. We know what a joy it is for dear friends to meet after a long period of separation. They demonstrate their love for each other in embraces, kisses, tears, and so on. What a day this will be, and how the pains, agonies, and groans at parting will be recompensed by the joy of such a meeting!

**Application**

*Lesson 1*

Since Christ was raised from the dead, death is overcome and swallowed up in victory. Death is a dreadful enemy. It defies all the sons and daughters of Adam. No one could deal with this king of terrors except Christ. By dying, He went into the dragon's den, fought with it, defeated it in its own territory and dominion, and emerged the conqueror. Death could not hold Him (Acts 2:24). Because Christ conquered death as our representative, we triumph over it as a vanquished enemy (1 Cor. 15:55). Our victory over death, obtained by Christ's resurrection, is twofold: (1) personal and incomplete and (2) general and complete. Christ actually overcame death at His resurrection, perfectly and virtually for us as our head. But at the general resurrection of the saints (which Christ's resurrection as the firstfruits guarantees) death will be utterly vanquished and destroyed. Until then, it exercises a little power over the bodies of the saints, in which respect it is called the "last enemy" (1 Cor. 15:26). Death holds our bodies in the grave until the coming of Christ, and then it will be utterly vanquished (v. 54). At that moment, the defeat of death will be fully completed in our persons, though it is already completed in Christ's. For the present, it smites with its dart but not with its sting, as the body remains for a time under it. But there is no reason why a believer should stand in slavish fear of it.

*Lesson 2*

Christ's resurrection has a powerful and comfortable influence upon the resurrection of the saints. It is, therefore, our duty to govern, dispose, and employ our bodies, as those who understand the glory that is prepared for us at the resurrection. First, we should use and employ our bodies for God. Many good duties are lost and spoiled by sinful indulgence to our bodies. We are generally more solicitous to live long than to live usefully. To have an able and healthy body, and not use it for God for fear of hurting it, is as if one should refuse to work or ride a strong and stately horse. Second, we should preserve the due honor of our bodies. We should possess them in "sanctification and honour" (1 Thess. 4:4). Eyes, which will see God, should not now be defiled with sin. Ears, which will hear the "hallelujahs" of the blessed, should not now be inlets to vanity. God has designed honor for our bodies. We must not, therefore, make them the instruments of sin (1 Cor. 3:17; 6:18). Third, we should not let the contentment and accommodation of our bodies draw our souls into snares, bringing them under the power of temptation. How many thousands of precious souls perish eternally for the satisfaction of the body but for a moment? Fourth, we should be quick to give to the refreshment of the saints whose present necessities require our assistance (Matt. 25:40; Luke 14:13–14).

*Lesson 3*

Christ is risen from the dead as a public person and representative of believers. Thus, we should be concerned to secure an interest in Christ and consequently in the blessed resurrection. What consolation is left in this world if the hope of the resurrection is taken away? It is this blessed hope that must support us under all the troubles of life and in the agonies of death. The securing of a blessed resurrection to ourselves is, therefore, the greatest concernment we have in this world. And we may secure it upon discovery of the following evidences.

First, we are born again. "Blessed be the God and Father of our Lord Jesus Christ, which according to his abundant mercy hath begotten us again unto a lively hope by the resurrection of Jesus Christ from the dead" (1 Peter 1:3). Christ's resurrection is the foundation of our hope, and the new birth is our title to it. Until our souls are partakers of the spiritual resurrection from the death of sin, we can have no assurance that our bodies will be partakers of that blessed resurrection to life. "Blessed and holy is he that hath part in the first resurrection: on such the second death hath no power" (Rev. 20:6). Unregenerate souls cannot expect a comfortable meeting with their bodies. They will rise at the sound of the last trumpet but not for the same end as the saints nor by the same principle as the saints. If the Holy Spirit is now a principle of sanctification in us, He will be the principle of a joyful resurrection. If we do not have a gracious soul now, we must not expect a glorious body then.

Second, we have died with Christ. "If we have been planted together in the likeness of his death, we shall be also in the likeness of his resurrection" (Rom. 6:5). In Scripture, we are said to suffer together and to be glorified together, to die together and to live together, to be crucified together and to be buried together. Each of these expressions denotes the communion we have with Christ in His death and life. Now, if the power of Christ's death (its mortifying influence) is upon our hearts (killing our lusts), then the power of His life (or resurrection) will come upon our dead bodies to revive and raise them up to live with Him in glory.

Third, our hearts and affections are with Christ in heaven. "For our conversation is in heaven; from whence also we look for the Saviour, the Lord Jesus Christ: who shall change our vile body, that it may be fashioned like unto his glorious body" (Phil. 3:20–21). The body is called "vile," not as God made it but as sin marred it. It is not "vile" absolutely in itself, but relatively in comparison to what it will be at the resurrection. At that time, our scattered bones and dispersed dust will be gathered and fashioned like Christ's glorious body. The evidence of our participation in this resurrection is that our conversation is already heavenly. The disposition of our souls is already so; therefore, the frame of our bodies in due time will be also.

Fourth, we strive now by any means to attain the resurrection of the dead. "If by any means I might attain unto the resurrection of the dead" (Phil. 3:11). The apostle does not simply mean a resurrection from the dead, for all people will attain that. He intends the complete holiness and perfection that will attend the state of the resurrection (v. 12). So then, if God has raised in our hearts a vehement desire and assiduous endeavor after a perfect freedom from sin and full conformity to God in the beauties of holiness, our present pantings speak us to be the people designed for it.

Fifth, we do good in our generation. If we are fruitful and useful in the world, we will have a part in the blessed resurrection. "All that are in the graves shall hear his voice, and shall come forth; they that have done good, unto the resurrection of life" (John 5:28–29). Now, it is not every materially good act that entitles a person to this privilege, but the matter, manner, and end must be good. What a spur should this be to us all! The apostle concludes the doctrine of the resurrection with this solemn exhortation: "Therefore, my beloved brethren, be ye stedfast, unmoveable, always abounding in the work of the Lord, forasmuch as ye know that your labour is not in vain in the Lord" (1 Cor. 15:58). Thanks be to God for His unspeakable gift!

# 18

# Christ's Ascension

*Jesus saith unto her, Touch me not; for I am not yet ascended to my Father: but go to my brethren, and say unto them, I ascend unto my Father, and your Father; and to my God, and your God.* —JOHN 20:17

In this sermon, we follow Christ into heaven, where He lodges Himself in the bosom of ineffable love and delight. It was His end in rising from the dead to live a most glorious life as an enthroned king in heaven. He indicates as much in His words to Mary: "Go to my brethren, and say unto them, I ascend unto my Father."

In the preceding verses, we read of Mary waiting beside Christ's grave, exceedingly troubled because she did not know what had become of Him (v. 15). Christ calls her by name, "Mary." Recognizing His voice, she turns to Him, "Rabboni," and (as a soul transported with joy) rushes into His arms. But Christ says, "Touch me not." It is strange that He, who was so kind and tender to all, and commanded Thomas to put his finger into His wounds, should forbid Mary to touch Him. It was not for a lack of love for her, but because He was not yet "ascended." There will be a time for embracing when we are in heaven.

Christ follows this command with another: "Go to my brethren, and say unto them, I ascend unto my Father." He describes His disciples as His "brethren." It is a sweet designation, full of love. His message for them is that He ascends to His Father. It is put in the present tense, as if He had been ascending, though He would not ascend for several weeks. He so expresses it to show what was the next part of His work—namely, to act in heaven for them. His heart was set upon it. "I ascend unto my Father, and your Father; and to my God, and your God." He does not mean that God is His and theirs in the same manner. God is the disciples' God by creation, and He is their Father by adoption and regeneration. He is Christ's God by right of creation and by special covenant and confederation. He is Christ's Father, in terms of His manhood, by predestination and by designation to the glorious office of mediator. He is also Christ's Father, in terms of His Godhead, by eternal generation. This is the substance of the comfortable message, sent by Mary to the pensive disciples.

*Doctrine: Christ did not only rise from the dead but also ascended into heaven, to dispatch all that remained to be done for the completion of the salvation of His people.*

"He that descended is the same also that ascended up far above all heavens, that he might fill all things" (Eph. 4:10; see Mark 16:19; Luke 24:51). This is sometimes called His going (John 16:7), being exalted (Acts 2:33), being "made higher than the heavens" (Heb. 7:26), and entering "within the veil"

(Heb. 6:19–20). These are synonymous phrases expressing His ascension.

Christ tells us in our verse, "I ascend." Although it was Christ's whole person that ascended, it was a figurative expression with respect to His divine nature. It was properly Christ's humanity that changed places and conditions. "I came forth from the Father, and am come into the world: again, I leave the world, and go to the Father" (John 16:28). He goes away, and we see Him no more. As God, He is still with us spiritually, even to the end of the world. But, as man, "the heaven must receive [him] until the times of restitution of all things" (Acts 3:21).

### The Place of Christ's Ascension

Christ ascended from this world. More particularly, it was from Mount Olivet, near Jerusalem, the very place where He began His final sorrowful tragedy. The place where His heart was formerly saddened is now the place where it is made glad. O what a different frame Christ was in on the mount before His passion and on the mount at His ascension! It is manifest that He ascended into the third heavens: the throne of God, where all the saints will be with Him forever. It is said to be far above all heavens (i.e., the heavens we can see). He is gone into His Father's house (John 14:2), to the place He was before (John 6:62), to that sweet and glorious bosom of love and delight, from where He came at His incarnation.

### The Time of Christ's Ascension

It was forty days after His resurrection. Christ's care for His people was manifested in His stay with them. Ineffable glory was prepared for Him in heaven, and awaiting His coming, but He would not possess it until He had settled all things here for the good of His church. During this time, He confirmed the truth of His resurrection and gave commands to the apostles concerning the order of His kingdom. This was needful because He intended for their "acts" to be the rules for future churches. When He had set all things in order, He stayed no longer. He had work of great concernment to do for us in heaven.

### The Manner of Christ's Ascension

First, Christ ascended *representatively*. He entered heaven as a forerunner in our names and upon our accounts (Heb. 6:20). This implies His public capacity. "I go to prepare a place for you" (John 14:2). He took possession of heaven in our names. He took possession of "mansions" and keeps them for our arrival. His entrance into heaven as our forerunner also implies His supremacy. He was the first to enter heaven directly and immediately in His own name and upon His own account. All the saints who died before Him entered heaven in His name.

Second, Christ ascended *triumphantly*. "God is gone up with a shout, the LORD with the sound of a trumpet. Sing praises to God, sing praises: sing praises unto our King, sing praises" (Ps. 47:5–6). A cloud is prepared as a royal chariot to carry up the King of Glory to His princely pavilion. "A cloud received him out of their sight" (Acts 1:9). A royal guard of mighty angels surrounded the chariot. What jubilations were heard in heaven! The whole city of God was moved at His coming. When God brought His Son into the world, He commanded all the angels to worship Him (Heb. 1:6). At

His return to His glory, having finished His work of redemption, there was no less celebration. "I saw in the night visions, and, behold, one like the Son of man came with the clouds of heaven, and came to the Ancient of days, and they brought him near before him. And there was given him dominion, and glory, and a kingdom, that all people, nations, and languages, should serve him" (Dan. 7:13–14). This vision was accomplished at Christ's ascension, when the angels brought Him to the Ancient of Days (i.e., God the Father), who expressed His welcome to Christ by giving Him glory and a kingdom. The Father received Him with open arms, rejoicing exceedingly to see Him again in heaven. Therefore, Christ was "received up into glory" (1 Tim. 3:16). He ascended and the Father received Him as no one has ever been received.

Third, Christ ascended *generously*. He gave His invaluable gifts to His church. "The chariots of God are twenty thousand, even thousands of angels: the Lord is among them, as in Sinai, in the holy place. Thou hast ascended on high, thou hast led captivity captive: thou hast received gifts for men; yea, for the rebellious also, that the LORD God might dwell among them" (Ps. 68:17–18; see Eph. 4:8). These words are a celebration of David's famous victory over God's enemies. They point to Christ, who overcame our enemies by His death on the cross and triumphed in His resurrection and ascension. He took the parts and gifts of His enemies and gave them to the church for its use and service. Thus, He received gifts, even for the rebellious—that is, He sanctifies the natural gifts and faculties of those who formerly hated His people, dedicating them to the Lord in His people's service. People of all sorts, greater and smaller, have been given to the church. Christ has given all sorts of offices (extraordinary and ordinary): prophets, apostles, evangelists, pastors, and teachers (Eph. 4:11–12). Thousands now in heaven, and thousands still on earth, bless Christ for His ascension gifts.

Fourth, Christ ascended *lovingly*. While He was blessing His people, He departed from them (Luke 24:50–51). And thus, "having loved his own which were in the world, he loved them unto the end" (John 13:1). Christ manifested a great deal of love in His last act in this world. Their last sight of Him was sweet and encouraging. They heard nothing from His lips but love and they saw nothing in His face but love until He mounted His triumphant chariot and was removed from their sight. Surely, these blessings were rich and sweet. As to their matter, they were the mercies that His blood had purchased for them. As to their extent, they reach to us as well as them. They stood as representatives of the future churches (Matt. 28:20). In blessing them, therefore, Christ blesses us. In this, we can be sure that Christ carried a heart full of love for us into heaven.

Fifth, Christ ascended *powerfully*. He was not passive in His ascension, but it was by His own act that He went to heaven (Acts 1:10). This clearly proves that He is God, for no mere creature ever ascended far above the heavens as Christ did.

### The Purpose of Christ's Ascension

Christ's ascension was necessary for many reasons. First, if He had not ascended, He could not intercede for us. If we take away Christ's intercession, we remove all hope. Without Christ as our advocate in heaven, what is there to comfort us when we sin?

Second, if Christ had not ascended, we could not enter heaven when we die. He went to "prepare a place" for us (John 14:2). He was the first to enter heaven directly and in His own name. If He had not done so, we could not enter when we die. The forerunner made way for all who follow Him. Our bodies cannot ascend at the resurrection but in the virtue of Christ's ascension, for He ascended in the capacity as our head to His Father and our Father.

Third, if Christ had not ascended, He could not have been installed in the glory He now enjoys in heaven. And then, how could the Father's promise be made good to Him?

Fourth, if Christ had not ascended, we could not be satisfied that His payment on the cross made full satisfaction to God. How is it that the Holy Spirit convinces the world of righteousness (John 16:9–10) but from Christ's going to the Father, which gives evidence of God's satisfaction with His person and work?

Fifth, if Christ had not ascended, we could not enjoy the great blessings of the Holy Spirit. If Christ had not gone away, the Comforter would not have come (v. 7). He begins where Christ finished, for He receives from Christ and shows it to us (v. 14). The Holy Spirit was not given prior to Christ's ascension in the same measure that He was given after Christ's ascension. By Christ's ascension, the Holy Spirit's sanctifying and ministering gifts were shed forth more commonly and abundantly. These fell from Christ when He ascended. Whatever good of conversion, edification, support, or comfort we receive from spiritual ordinances, the Holy Spirit has shed it forth. It is the fruit of Christ's ascension.

It was for His glory and our advantage that Christ ascended. "If ye loved me, ye would rejoice, because I said, I go unto the Father: for my Father is greater than I" (John 14:28). When He ascended, we lost the comfort of His bodily presence. But we rejoice because it is for our benefit as well as His glory. He has ascended to His Father and our Father, to His God and our God. From there, He bestows those blessings for which His people are not troubled over His departure (v. 1).

## Application

*Lesson 1*

Christ ascended into heaven. He is our treasure; therefore, our hearts should be in heaven. It is not good if our love and our Lord are in two different countries. We ascended *virtually* with Him when He ascended. We will ascend *personally* on a future day. In the meantime, we ought to ascend *spiritually* to Him in acts of faith, love, and desire. It would be good if we could say with the apostle, "Our conversation is in heaven; from whence also we look for the Saviour" (Phil. 3:20). An ascended heart is the best evidence of our interest in Christ's ascension.

*Lesson 2*

Christ entered heaven as a forerunner. We should be diligent in following Him. Did He run to glory, and will we linger? Did He fly as an eagle toward heaven, and will we creep like snails? "Let us lay aside every weight, and the sin which doth so easily beset us, and let us run with patience the race that is set before us, looking unto Jesus" (Heb. 12:1–2). The Captain of our salvation has entered within the gates of the new Jerusalem and calls to us out of heaven to hasten to Him, proposing the greatest encouragements to those who are following after Him: "To him that overcometh will I grant to sit with me in my throne, even as I also overcame, and am set down with my Father in his throne" (Rev. 3:21).

*Lesson 3*

Christ ascended triumphantly, leading captivity captive. We have little reason to fear our conquered enemies. Sin, Satan, and every enemy were led away in triumph, dragged at Christ's chariot wheels, brought after Him (as it were) in chains. It is a lovely sight to see the necks of those tyrants under the foot of our Joshua. He made "a shew of them openly" (Col. 2:15). Their strength is broken forever. In this He showed Himself to be more than a conqueror. He triumphed too. Christ trod Satan under His feet, and He has promised to tread him under our feet as well (Rom. 16:20). Our enemies retain some power at present. The serpent may yet bruise our heel, but Christ has crushed his head.

*Lesson 4*

Christ ascended bountifully, shedding forth many mercies upon His people. We must be careful not to abuse Christ's precious ascension gifts, but value them as the choicest mercies. These gifts are the ordinances and officers of the church and the Holy Spirit who furnished the church with all its gifts. We must not abuse either of these. At His ascension, Christ sent the Holy Spirit from heaven to make up for His bodily absence. This gift is a great pledge of His tender care for His people. We must take heed not to vex Him by our disobedience, nor grieve Him by our unkindnesses, nor quench Him by our sinful neglect of duty. We should deal kindly with the Holy Spirit, yielding up ourselves to His guidance and conduct. To persuade us to this, let me suggest a few considerations.

First, the Holy Spirit was the first and principal mercy that Christ received for us upon entering heaven. "I will pray the Father, and he shall give you another Comforter, that he may abide with you" (John 14:16). As soon as He had set foot there, He asked the Father to dispatch the Holy Spirit and send Him down to His people. The Holy Spirit is the firstborn of all mercies; therefore, He deserves first place in our hearts.

Second, the Holy Spirit does not come to us in His own name but in the name of the Father and the Son. "But when the Comforter is come, whom I will send unto you from the Father" (John 15:26; see also John 14:26). He is the messenger who comes from both of these great and holy persons. If we have any love for God who made us and Christ who redeemed us, we will show our love for the Holy Spirit by obeying Him.

Third, the Holy Spirit deserves our devotion on His own account. (1) On account of His nature. He is God, coequal with the Father and Son in nature and dignity. "The Spirit of the LORD spake by me, and his word was in my tongue. The God of Israel said, the Rock of Israel spake to me" (2 Sam. 23:2–3). The Spirit of the LORD, the God of Israel, and the Rock of Israel are one. The Holy Spirit is God. He is omnipotent, for He created all things (Gen. 1:2). He is omnipresent, for He fills all things (Ps. 139:7). He is omniscient, for He knows all things (Rom. 9:1). If, therefore, we grieve Him, we grieve God. (2) On account of His office. He comes to us as an advocate to assist us in prayer (Rom. 8:26). He comes to us as a comforter (John 14:16). His work is to take what is Christ's and show it to us—that is, to take His death, resurrection, ascension, and intercession and show them to us. It was He who formed Christ's body in the womb and so prepared Him to be a sacrifice for us. He filled Christ's humanity with His fullness, thereby fitting and anointing Him for the discharge of His office. It is He who puts efficacy into the ordinances. It is He who blessed them to our conviction and conversion. It is He who is the bond of union between Christ and our souls, without which we could never have communion with Christ. It is He who has helped our infirmities when we did not know what to pray, comforted our hearts when we did not know what to do, preserved us from sin and ruin when we have been on the slippery brink. It is He who (in His sanctifying work) is the best evidence of our right to heaven. His mercies are endless. O grieve not the Holy Spirit whom Christ sent, as soon as He went to heaven, to perform all these offices for us!

*Lesson 5*

Christ ascended to the Father as our forerunner. The door of salvation stands open to all believers. By virtue of Christ's ascension, we will ascend far above the visible heavens. O what a splendid habitation has He provided for us! "God is not ashamed to be called their God: for he hath prepared for them a city" (Heb. 11:16; see John 14:2). Such is the love that Christ has for each believer that He would have built that house for him alone. May God give us a joyful meeting with our forerunner! And, in the meantime, may the love of our Savior inflame our hearts so that whenever we cast a look toward that place, we may say with melting affections, "Blessed be God for His unspeakable gift!"

# 19

# Christ's Present Session

*When he had by himself purged our sins, [he] sat down*
*on the right hand of the Majesty on high.*
—HEBREWS 1:3

Having ascended to heaven, Christ sits down in the seat of
honor and rest. It is a seat of honor because His Father prepared it for Him at His right hand. It is a seat of rest because
all His enemies are as a footstool under His feet. With this
exaltation, Christ's condition is changed dramatically. While
here on earth, He groaned, labored, suffered, sweat, wept,
and found no rest. When He entered heaven, He entered into
rest. He sits upon the highest throne, prepared for Him by
His Father. "Who being the brightness of his glory, and the
express image of his person, and upholding all things by the
word of his power, when he had by himself purged our sins,
sat down on the right hand of the Majesty on high." Christ is
described in three ways in this verse.

First, He is described by His essential and eternal glory
and dignity: He is "the brightness of his glory." This designation points to His eternal and ineffable generation. He is

"light of light" (as the Nicene Creed expresses it). This designation also reminds us that as the sun communicates its light and influence to us by its beams, so God communicates His goodness and manifests Himself to us by Christ. He is also "the express image [or character] of his person." This expression does not refer to the impressed image of a seal upon wax but to the engraving in the seal itself.

Second, Christ is described by His work: "when he had by himself purged our sins." He accomplished this here on earth in His humbled state. It was a glorious work.

Third, Christ is described by the glory that was the reward of His work: He "sat down on the right hand of the Majesty on high." That is to say, the Lord clothed Him with the greatest power and highest honor that heaven could afford. This is what the phrase "the right hand of the Majesty" imports.

*Doctrine: When Christ had finished His work on earth, He was placed in the seat of highest honor and authority at the right hand of God in heaven.*

This truth is transformingly glorious. Christ's high advancement was foretold before He took the work of redemption in hand. "The LORD said unto my Lord, Sit thou at my right hand, until I make thine enemies thy footstool" (Ps. 110:1). This promise was fulfilled in Christ, after His resurrection and ascension, in His supreme exaltation far above all created beings in heaven and earth (Eph. 1:20–22). We will here consider two things.

## What Is God's Right Hand?

God does not have physical hands. The expression "right hand" is figurative, whereby God stoops to our limited understanding, in order to convey three things.

First, the right hand is the place of *honor*. This is why Solomon placed his mother in a seat at his right hand (1 Kings 2:19). God sets Christ at His right hand, thereby lavishing favor and honor upon Him. "But to which of the angels said he at any time, Sit on my right hand?" (Heb. 1:13).

Second, the right hand is a place of *power*. The setting of Christ in this position imports His exaltation to the highest authority and most supreme dominion. This does not mean that God the Father advanced Christ above Himself (1 Cor. 15:27). It means that Christ sits as an enthroned king at God's right hand and that He possesses the most sovereign and supreme power. "Hereafter shall ye see the Son of man sitting on the right hand of power" (Matt. 26:64).

Third, the right hand is a place of *nearness*. "The Lord at thy right hand shall strike through kings in the day of his wrath" (Ps. 110:5)—that is, the Lord, who is very near to you, will subdue your enemies.

## What Does It Mean for Christ to Sit at God's Right Hand?

First, it implies the perfecting and completing of Christ's work. After His work was finished, He sat down and rested from His labors. "And every priest standeth daily ministering and offering oftentimes the same sacrifices, which can never take away sins: but this man, after he had offered one sacrifice for sins for ever, sat down on the right hand of God" (Heb. 10:11–12). The Old Testament priests stand daily because their sacrifices cannot take away sin. But Christ fully accomplished His work by one offering; hence, He sits (rests) in heaven forever.

Second, Christ's sitting down at God's right hand proclaims the Father's delight and satisfaction in Him and His work. "The LORD said unto my Lord, Sit thou at my right hand" (Ps. 110:1). These are the Father's words as He welcomes Christ to heaven. It is as if He had said, "O, My Son, what will be done for You this day? You have finished a great work, and in every way have proved Yourself to be an able and faithful servant. What honors will I now bestow upon You? The highest glory in heaven is not too high for You. Come, sit at My right hand." O how well pleased the Father is with Christ! He delighted greatly to behold Him in His work on earth (John 10:17; 2 Peter 1:17). It was a work that the heart of God had been set upon from eternity. He took infinite delight in it.

Third, Christ's sitting down at God's right hand marks the advancement of His human nature to the highest honor—even to be the object of adoration for angels and saints. It is properly His human nature that is the subject of all this honor and advancement. Being advanced to the right hand of Majesty, it has become an object of worship and adoration—not simply as it is flesh and blood but as it is personally united to the second person and enthroned in the supreme glory of heaven. O here is the mystery! Flesh and blood are advanced to the highest throne of majesty and installed in that glory. We may now direct our worship to Him as God-man. To this end was His humanity so advanced that it might be adored and worshiped by all. The Father will accept no honor divided from Christ's honor. "He that honoureth not the Son honoureth not the Father which hath sent him"

(John 5:22–23). Hence, the apostles, in the salutations in their epistles, always pray for grace, mercy, and peace, from God the Father and our Lord Jesus Christ.

Fourth, Christ's sitting down at God's right hand imports the sovereignty and supremacy of Christ over all. When the Father said to Him, "Sit at my right hand," He delivered to Him the dispensation of the kingdom, and He put the scepter of government into His hand. "He must reign, till he hath put all enemies under his feet" (1 Cor. 15:25; see also Heb. 2:7–8). Christ is Lord over the spiritual kingdom, the church (Matt. 28:18–20). He is also Lord over the providential kingdom, the world (Ps. 110:2). And His providential kingdom is subordinate to His spiritual kingdom, meaning He rules and orders the first for the benefit and advantage of the second (Eph. 1:22).

Fifth, Christ's sitting down at God's right hand implies that Christ has conquered His enemies. They are under His feet, implying perfect conquest and complete victory. It is true that His victory has not yet been consummated, but He is crowned with glory (Heb. 2:8–9). This shows that His enemies' power is now broken. Though they oppose Him at present, it is to no purpose at all, for He is so infinitely above them that they must fall before Him. Christ is at God's right hand, meaning God's power stands ready to strike His enemies (Ps. 110:5).

Sixth, Christ's sitting down at God's right hand notes the great and wonderful change that occurred in His condition. It is far different than it was in the days of His humiliation on earth. O what a wonderful change heaven has made in Him! It is good to compare His humiliation and exaltation together. He was born in a stable, but now He reigns in His royal palace.

He had a manger for His cradle, but now He sits on a chair of state. Oxen and donkeys were His companions, but now multitudes of saints and angels minister around His throne. He was held in contempt, but now He has obtained a more excellent name than angels. He did not have a place to lay His head, but now He is heir of all things. He had no beauty that we should desire Him, but now the beauty of His countenance sends forth glorious beams that dazzle the eyes of all the celestial inhabitants. Here He sweated, but there He sits. Here He groaned, but there He triumphs. Here He lay upon the ground, but there He sits on the throne of glory.

Seventh, Christ's sitting at God's right hand implies the advancement of believers to the highest honor. His present session concerns us because He sits there as our representative. In this sense, we are seated with Him in the heavenly places (Eph. 2:6). This is our hope and confidence. We have an interest in the flesh and blood of Christ that is now exalted. Therefore, where He reigns, we will reign; where He is glorified, we will be glorified. Surely it is a matter of exceeding joy to believe that Christ, our head (flesh and blood), is in all this glory at His Father's right hand.

## Application

*Lesson 1*

It is a great honor for Christ to sit enthroned at God's right hand. There is an honor reserved in heaven for those who are faithful to Christ. Christ prayed, "Father, I will that they also, whom thou hast given me, be with me where I am; that they may behold my glory, which thou hast given me" (John 17:24). "Thine eyes shall see the king in his beauty" (Isa. 33:17).

This promise respected Hezekiah in type but Christ in truth. We will not only see Christ on His throne but sit with Him enthroned in glory. This sight of Christ will change us into His likeness (1 John 3:2). He will place us (as it were) on His throne with Him (2 Tim. 2:12; Rev. 3:21). The Father set Christ at His right hand, and Christ will set us on His right hand. O what manner of love is this!

These promises do not mean that we will have a higher glory than Christ or that we will have an equal glory with Christ, for in all things He must have the preeminence. But we note the great honor that Christ will put upon us, that His glory will be our glory in heaven (2 Thess. 1:10). And so it will be a social glory. O it is admirable to think where free grace has placed poor dust and ashes! "Beloved, now are we the sons of God, and it doth not yet appear what we shall be: but we know that, when he shall appear, we shall be like him; for we shall see him as he is" (1 John 3:2). O what reason we have to honor Christ on earth when He is preparing such honor for us in heaven!

*Lesson 2*

Since Christ is enthroned in heaven, it is impossible for His interest to miscarry on earth. The church has many subtle and potent enemies. But as Haman could not prevail against the Jews while Esther spoke for them to the king, so our enemies cannot prevail against us while Christ sits at the Father's right hand. Will He allow His enemies, who are under His feet, to touch the very apple of His eye (Zech. 2:8)? "He must reign, till he hath put all enemies under his feet" (1 Cor. 15:25). The enemies under His feet will not destroy the children in

His arms. He sits in heaven on purpose, to manage all to the advantage of His church (Eph. 1:22). Are our enemies powerful? Our King sits on the right hand of power. Are they subtle in their plots and plans? Our King overrules all that they do. "He that sitteth in the heavens shall laugh: the LORD shall have them in derision" (Ps. 2:4). He might permit them to harass us, but it will be for our enlargement. He might allow them to distress us, but it will be recompensed with inward mercies. The opposition of Christ's enemies occasions singular benefit to His people.

*Lesson 3*
Christ is set down at the right hand of the Majesty in heaven. We should, therefore, approach Him with reverence in the duties of His worship. We must discard low thoughts of Christ; formal and careless frames in praying, hearing, and receiving; and deadness and drowsiness in duties. He is a great king. In comparison to Him, all the kings of the earth are little bits of clay. Even the angels cover their faces in His presence. When John had a vision of this enthroned King, it was so overpowering that he fell at His feet as dead (Rev. 1:17). O we serve and worship a glorious Lord! Surely He is greatly to be feared in the assembly of His saints and to be held in reverence by all who draw near to Him. There is indeed a boldness and liberty of speech allowed to the saints (Eph. 3:12). We may indeed come to Him as the children of a king come to their father. This double relation causes a due mixture of love and reverence in our hearts. We may be free, but not rude, in His presence. Though He is our Father, Brother, Friend, there remains a distance between Him and us that is infinite.

*Lesson 4*

Christ is gloriously advanced to the highest throne. We do not need to consider ourselves dishonored when we suffer the vilest things for His sake. The very chains and sufferings of Christ have glory in them; hence, Moses esteemed "the reproach of Christ greater riches than the treasures in Egypt" (Heb. 11:26). He saw an excellence in the worst of Christ's reproaches that made him forsake earthly honors and riches. He did not only endure the reproaches of Christ but counted them treasures. Surely there is a little paradise in suffering for Christ. If we consider how exceedingly kind Christ is to those who count it their glory to be abased for Him, it would make us love His reproaches.

# 20

# Christ's Triumphant Return

*And he commanded us to preach unto the people, and to testify that it is he which was ordained of God to be the Judge of quick and dead.* —ACTS 10:42

Christ is enthroned in the highest glory in heaven for the effectual and successful government of the world and church, until all those (given to Him by the Father and purchased by His blood) are gathered. After this, the great day of judgment will come, when the precious will be separated from the vile. Christ will then deliver up the kingdom to His Father so that "God may be all in all" (1 Cor. 15:28).

This last act, Christ's judging the world, is a special part of His exaltation. The Father "hath given him authority to execute judgment also, because he is the Son of man" (John 5:27). In that day, His glory as absolute Lord and King will shine forth as the sun when it shines in its full strength. It will be a great honor to Christ, who stood arraigned and condemned at Pilate's bar, to sit upon the great white throne, surrounded with thousands and thousands of angels and with all people waiting upon Him to receive the final sentence from

His mouth. The glory of Christ's power and sovereignty will be eminently and illustriously displayed before all. And this is the great truth that He commanded to be preached: "that it is he which was ordained of God to be the Judge of quick and dead." There are several noteworthy details in this verse.

First, the *subject* of this authority: Christ. He is ordained to be Judge. Judgment is the act of the whole Trinity. The Father and the Spirit judge as well as Christ in respect of authority and consent. But it is Christ's act in respect of visible management and execution. And so it is His because the Father has conferred it upon Him as the Son of man. But it is not His so as to exclude either the Father or the Spirit from their authority, for they judge through Him.

Second, the *object* of this authority: "the quick and dead." This includes everyone who is alive at His coming or who lived prior to His coming. It also includes all the apostate angels that fell from heaven and are reserved in chains for this great day. Their actions, both secret and open, are the focus of this judgment (Rom. 2:16; 2 Cor. 5:5).

Third, the *source* of this authority: God the Father. He has "ordained" Christ to be the judge. Christ is appointed, as the Son of man, to this honorable work and office. The word notes a firm establishment of Christ in that office by His Father. He is now, by right of redemption, Lord and King. He enacts laws for government, then He comes to judge people for their obedience and disobedience to His laws.

*Doctrine: Christ is ordained by God the Father to be the judge of the living and the dead.*

This truth stands upon the authority of Scripture. We have it from Christ's own mouth: "The Father judgeth no man, but hath committed all judgment unto the Son" (John 5:22). And so the apostle declares, "[God] hath appointed a day, in the which he will judge the world in righteousness by that man whom he hath ordained; whereof he hath given assurance unto all men, in that he hath raised him from the dead" (Acts 17:31; see also Rom. 2:16). How can we be certain there is a future judgment?

First, the true and faithful sayings of God plainly reveal it, while the justice and righteousness of God require it. "Shall not the Judge of all the earth do right?" (Gen. 18:25). Righteousness itself requires that a difference be made between the righteous and the wicked (Isa. 3:10). But no such distinction is fully made in this world. Oftentimes, the wicked prosper while the righteous perish (Eccl. 7:15; Hab. 1:13). Therefore, the wise man justly infers a judgment to come: "And moreover I saw under the sun the place of judgment, that wickedness was there; and the place of righteousness, that iniquity was there. I said in mine heart, God shall judge the righteous and the wicked: for there is a time there for every purpose and for every work" (Eccl. 3:16–17; see also James 5:6–7).

Second, people are reasonable creatures, and every reasonable creature is an accountable creature. We are capable of moral government. Our actions have a relation to a law. We are swayed by rewards and punishments. We act by counsel and, therefore, we must expect to give an account for our actions (Rom. 14:12). Moreover, God has entrusted gifts of body, mind, estate, time, and so on to us. A time to render an account for all these will come (Matt. 25:14–15). We are stewards, and stewards must give an account.

Third, our conscience testifies to the certainty of judgment. It is a truth engraved on each person's heart. We have a little tribunal in our conscience, which accuses and excuses for good and evil. It could never do this if there were not a future judgment. In this court, records are kept of all we do. But if there is no judgment, then why the need for records? Some vainly imagine that this is merely the fruit of education and upbringing. But if it were, it would not be so universal. Who could be the author of such a common deception? It is evident that the consciences of the heathen have these offices of accusing and excusing (Rom. 2:15). And it is hard to imagine that some undefined influence could induce so many doubts, fears, and troubles among them and interrupt the whole course of their corrupt living. There is a conscience and, therefore, it is beyond doubt that a day of judgment is coming.

### The Manner of Judgment

What will it be like? First, it will be a *solemn* judgment. It is called the "judgment of the great day" (Jude 6). Christ will break out of heaven with the shout of angels (1 Thess. 4:16–17). After this shout, the trump of God will sound. By this tremendous blast, sinners will be frightened out of their graves. But it will not carry any terror for the saints. Being raised, all will gather before the great throne on which Christ sits in glory. Adam's numerous offspring will stand before the Judge. Christ will "judge the secrets of men" (Rom. 2:16). He will separate the tares from the wheat and sentence all to their everlasting states. O what a solemn thing is this! The heart cannot conceive what impressions Christ's voice will make upon believers and unbelievers. (1) Imagine Christ upon His glorious throne, surrounded with myriads of angels. A poor, trembling unbeliever stands before Him. An exact scrutiny is made of his heart and life. The dreadful sentence is given. And then he cries as he is delivered to the executioners of eternal vengeance, never again to see a glimpse of hope or mercy. (2) Imagine Christ, like the general of an army, mentioning all the services that the saints have done for Him in this world. Then He justifies them by open proclamation. Then they enter through the gates of the city of God in that noble train of saints and angels. And so they are forever with the Lord. O what a great day this will be!

Second, it will be an *exact* judgment. Christ is a searcher of hearts. He has eyes as flames of fire (Rev. 1:14), which pierce to the inner man. "Every idle word that men shall speak, they shall give account thereof in the day of judgment" (Matt. 12:36). No hypocrite will escape. Justice holds the balance in an even hand.

Third, it will be a *universal* judgment. "We must all appear before the judgment seat of Christ" (2 Cor. 5:10; see also Rom. 14:12). Rich, poor, father, child, master, servant, believer, and unbeliever must stand forth in that day. "And I saw the dead, small and great, stand before God; and the books were opened" (Rev. 20:12).

Fourth, it will be a *final* judgment. There will be no appeal. This judgment is supreme and imperial, for Christ is "the blessed and only Potentate" (1 Tim. 6:15). Once the sentence is passed, its execution is infallible.

**The Appointment to Judgment**

In ordaining Christ to be the judge, God has highly exalted Him. This is very much to His honor. First, this act of judging pertains properly to His kingly office. Christ will be glorified as much in His kingly office as He has been in His other offices. This office will shine in its glory as the sun shines in the midst of the heavens.

Second, this act of judging will display His glory before the whole world. All the inhabitants of heaven, earth, and hell will be present at once before Him. Before this great assembly Christ will appear in royal majesty. "He shall come to be glorified in his saints, and to be admired in all them that believe" (2 Thess. 1:10). The inhabitants of the three regions (heaven, earth, and hell) will then rejoice or tremble before Him and acknowledge Him to be the supreme Lord and King.

Third, this act of judging will remove the reproach of His death. Pilate, Herod, and the high priest will now stand quivering before Him. The soldiers who abused Him, and the priests who reviled Him, will stand with trembling knees before His throne. "Every eye shall see him, and they also which pierced him" (Rev. 1:7). O what a contemptible person was Christ in their eyes! But now the brightness of His glory and the beams of His majesty will be such that the wicked will not stand in His presence. This will be a full and universal vindication of the death of Christ from all the contempt that attended it.

## Application

*Lesson 1*

Believers are certain they will not be condemned on the day when Christ judges the living and the dead. If believers are condemned in judgment, then Christ must give sentence against them. But He will not give a sentence of condemnation against them. Why not? First, He died to save them, and He will never overthrow the purpose of His own death. Second, they have already been cleared and absolved (Rom. 8:1). Therefore, they can never be condemned. One divine sentence cannot rescind another. Surely Christ will not retract His own word. Third, most of them will have passed their particular judgment long before that day and will have been admitted into heaven upon account of their justification. It cannot be imagined that Christ would now condemn them with the world. Fourth, God has judged them in their head, husband, friend, and brother, who loved them and gave Himself for them. They are already seated with Him in the heavenly places. The business of that day will not be to condemn them but to pronounce them pardoned and justified (Matt. 12:32; Acts 3:19). It will be a time of refreshing for God's people. We who believe will not come into condemnation (John 5:24; 1 Cor. 11:31–32).

*Lesson 2*

It will be miserable for unbelievers in that day when Christ judges the living and the dead. They will be speechless, helpless, and hopeless. Their hands will hang down and their knees will knock together. O what pale faces, quivering lips, fainting hearts, and roaring consciences will be among them on that day! Who will endure this day but those who by union with Christ are secured against its danger and dread?

Do you think it is possible to avoid appearing before God's throne? How can you imagine it? Is not the same power that revives your dust able to bring you before the throne? "We must all appear" (2 Cor. 5:10). It is not your choice to obey this summons or not.

Do you think there are no accusers or witnesses who will appear against you in God's court? Do you not think Satan will be there? What about your own conscience? Is it not privy to your secret wickedness? If it whispers now, it will thunder then (Rom. 2:15–16). Will not the Holy Spirit accuse you for resisting His motions and stifling thousands of His convictions? Will not your companions in sin accuse you? Will not your teachers be your accusers? Will not your relations be your accusers, especially those whom you have failed in all your relational duties? Will not everyone whom you have abused, defrauded, and mistreated be your accusers? It is without dispute that there will be plenty of accusers who appear against you.

Do you think you will be able to plead innocence as you stand before your accuser, Jesus Christ? Will you confess or deny the charge? If you confess, what is left? If you deny, your Judge (who searches hearts) will reveal the secrets of your heart. It will be of no use to lie. He knows all things. Lying will only add to your guilt.

Do you think there is something that will delay the execution of Christ's sentence? Do you hope He will be too merciful to judge you? You err if you expect to find mercy other than in the way He dispenses it. There will be numerous people who magnify His mercy on that day. They are those who obeyed His call, repented, believed, and obtained union with His person here. But it is against the settled law of Christ and constitution of the gospel to show mercy to the despisers of mercy. Perhaps you think your tears, cries, and pleadings will move Him. They are too late. "Many will say to me in that day, Lord, Lord, have we not prophesied in thy name? and in thy name have cast out devils? and in thy name done many wonderful works? And then will I profess unto them, I never knew you: depart from me, ye that work iniquity" (Matt. 7:22–23).

*Lesson 3*

Those who hope to be found in Christ must avoid sin and pursue godliness. First, we must be meek and patient under all injuries and abuses for Christ's sake. We do not avenge ourselves, but leave it to the Lord. "Be patient therefore, brethren, unto the coming of the Lord" (James 5:7). Second, we must be public-hearted Christians, seeking to minister to the distressed members of Christ's body. If we do, we will have a full reward in that day (Matt. 25:34–35). Third, we must be sober and watchful. We must keep the golden bridle of moderation upon all our affections and see that we are not overcharged with the cares of this present life (Luke 21:34–35). "Let your moderation be known unto all men. The Lord is at hand" (Phil. 4:5). Fourth, we must be diligent and careful to improve all that our Master has entrusted to us (Matt. 25:14–18). Fifth, we must be sincere in our profession. Our hearts must be found in God's statutes that we may never be ashamed. Nothing is so secret that it will remain hidden on that day.

# Conclusion

Reader, in a little while, you will come to the last day of your life. Do you have an interest in this blessed Redeemer? There is no sadder sight than a poor, Christless sinner shivering upon the brink of eternity. "Lord, what will become of me?" That this may not be your case, reflect upon what you have read in these sermons. Judge yourself in the light of them. Obey the calls of the Holy Spirit in them. Let not your slight and formal spirit float upon the surface of these truths, like a feather upon the water. Get them deeply fixed upon your soul by the Spirit of the Lord, turning them into life and power within you, so animating the whole course of your life that it may proclaim that you are one who esteems everything as dross that you may win Christ.